SO...
YOU CALL YOURSELF
A LEADER?

4 STEPS TO BECOMING
ONE WORTH FOLLOWING

BY KENNETH N. SIEGEL

©2004 Priority Imprints

ISBN: 0-9752750-0-3

Library of Congress Control Number: 2004102665

Cover by Mark Dame

Layout by Francine Smith

Submit all requests for reprinting to:
Greenleaf Book Group LLC
4425 Mopac South, Suite 600
Longhorn Bldg., 3rd Floor
Austin, TX 78735
(512) 891-6100

Published in the United States by
Priority Imprints
Beverly Hills, CA

Dedication

....

Dedicated to: My Wonderfully Supportive Parents, Who taught me
the power of **I**rreverence,
Passion and **C**ourage
And
My incredibly special family—whom I love dearly
Maren, Alex, Lauren, and Matthew
Who always show me how to
Get and stay R-E-A-L!

Acknowledgements

....

Since so many people have educated, supported, and personally enriched me and this work, I shall take great pleasure in acknowledging them accordingly, knowing I have inadvertently omitted some of them, to you my apologies.

This work owes whatever intellectual tradition it may contain to the late Shelly Duval of USC, Dick Ashmore and George Atwood at Rutgers, and Warren Bennis of the world, respectively. In their own unique ways, each has contributed a depth of perception and intellectual breadth which has made this work possible. Your ideas live on, as does your influence, and I thank you all.

At the professional level, so many clients have taught me so much more than I have taught them, that admitting so would require a refund of my consulting fees. The rather impressive executives at Avnet, Inc. including Roy Vallee, Rick Hamada, Harley Feldberg, Ed Kamins, Andy Bryant, Phil Gallagher, Steve Church, and many others have taught me the value of really applying what you study… and the difficulty of doing so. Their perseverance in the face of adversity and their willingness to take the journey with me are truly special.

Jon Epstein, Tom O'Riordan, Lou Spagna, Adrian Thomas, all CEO's who, at some level have always been R-E-A-L, have also been instrumental in my growth and development. Thank you for helping me grow.

And, at another level, are those special people who transcend all three categories: intellectual, personal, and professional. George Oliva, my manager, has been a pillar of strength and the staunchest advocate over a long period of time. There are not enough words to express my appreciation for his loyalty, his dedication, and his advocacy. Rich Ward, the enigma of enigmas, continues to impress me, and John Llewellyn, my most unlikely (yet, in many ways, deepest) friend and long-term ally always challenges and makes me better.

Lastly, at a hugely practical, yet ultimately indispensable level, are my writing partner, Keith Hollihan and my "personal" manager, Susan Guest. Keith's brilliance, creativity and empathic connectivity, along with his superb literary skills, served as the foundation for a very special collaborative effort. I hope to do it again…soon.

Susan, on the other hand, with her unsurpassed technical and organization skills, coupled with her kindness and willingness to help, made it possible for me to work and complete a book simultaneously. Thank you, SuzyQ.

To all of you, I say, what lies in your hands would never have been possible without you. I honor you all!

Table of Contents

....

....

Are We Ready for REAL* Leadership?

* **R**esponsible
  Empowering
  Accountable
  Loving

The Bottom Line of Business Leadership
(And, this time, we mean it.)

Business leaders understand the language of the bottom line. So, here's a bottom line assessment of our leadership needs today:

- The demand is immense
- The repositories are barren
- Trust accounts are dangerously depleted
- Credibility ratings have achieved near junk status
- Prospects for earning future followers are gloomy

How much lower can confidence in corporate leadership plunge? Top executives have appeared before congress to explain how they let billions of dollars and thousands of jobs evaporate while lining their own pockets. CEOs and CFOs are now required by law to swear that their glossy annual reports don't belong on the fiction shelves. Even Jack Welch, the icon of successful business leadership, has experienced a fall from grace—not because he lost any credibility as a manager, but because the extent of his own self-interest was so publicly exposed during his messy divorce.

Enron, Adelphia, Rite-Aid, Tyco, HealthSouth, Martha Stewart, Putnam Investments, Freddie Mac, WorldCom… although many paint those collapses as *accounting* scandals, we all know they were really *accountability* scandals. After all, companies didn't cause those atrocities of trust, *people* did. And not just any people, but the people at the top— those supposedly noble leaders who the people below looked to for inspiration, guidance, support, and example.

How widespread a problem do we actually face? Should we subscribe to the "few bad apples" theory and risk taking another bite? Or, should we start looking for a "new brand" of leader who's willing to take a longer, deeper, more honest look at themselves, and do the hard work of becoming someone really worth following?

As a corporate psychologist working with top executives and managers at Fortune 500 companies for the last twenty-five years, I've seen my share of abuses of trust, power, and human decency. From my perspective, none of the recent revelations about leadership have been surprising.

Although many leaders are quick to focus others on the bottom line, few would even think to hold themselves to the same standard. No executive or manager, for instance, has ever asked me to help them become a leader worth following—not at first, anyway. Instead, I am called in because their organization is in "distress," their people are "inadequate," or their key functions are "incapable" of working together as a team. Of course, it's never the leader's "fault." After all, "the buck stops here" is a saying that has taken on an entirely different meaning given today's standards for compensating executives.

But I know who pays *my* fee, so I listen carefully to the aforementioned problems and take detailed notes. Then, I go out into the hallways and examine the organizational distress, talk to those inadequate people, and check out those dysfunctional functions. And when I come back, I've got a whole lot of bad news to deliver.

Though the details may vary from case to case, the essence is basically the same. The organization, division, or work group is in distress because its leader is. Whether the executive or manager is aware of this or not (and usually they're the last to see the truth), no one really admires them as a leader, let alone thinks that he is worth following. Instead, the executive or manager's followers have lost emotional commitment to the job, and become actively engaged in undermining them. And why not? Those people, after all, have been ordered around, deceived, held back, manipulated, bullied, and not listened to for a long time. Any other emotional reaction—like passion, energy, commitment, or creative engagement—would be downright pathological.

My news, in the form of what managers call "feedback," always takes a while to sink in. I have learned to listen calmly to the excuses, the "poor me's" and baffled "how come's" that inevitably pour forth in self-defense. I try to turn the outward focused blame and denial into the tiniest wedge of self-awareness. I do so knowing that sometimes it only takes a little leverage, albeit accurately applied, to move a big mountain.

There is hope, and that's what keeps me going. There is also much work yet to be done, and that's why I've written this book.

Working with managers or executives, I help them to see the truth: They are not God's gifts to leadership excellence, but individuals reliant on the people around them to make a difference in the world. Together we peel back the covers on motivations and intentions to reveal what's really going on below the surface during the day-to-day circus of management—all those capricious orders, evasions of truth, ineffective decisions, and self-serving acts. In a flash of insight, we come to an understanding that the technical skills that got them to where they are today have nothing to do with the human skills they need now and in the future. Little by little, if they're lucky, brutally honest with themselves, and willing to change more than they think possible, they learn how to "become a leader worth following"—a person who works constantly on developing their inner strength, who demonstrates caring and sensitivity to those around them, who inspires those people to greater heights, and who ultimately makes their corner of the world a better place.

From the beginning, all along the way, and especially at the end, I remind them: "I never said this would be easy. But that doesn't mean it's not worth doing."

It's an uphill battle. Becoming a leader worth following is *hard work*. It requires courage, determination, openness, irreverence, passion, and a willingness to question ourselves as deeply as we are willing and eager to question others. Most leadership books assume that leaders are already engaging in some amount of genuine self-assessment and have a base level of self-knowledge as a result. In my experience, they do not. And so this book, and the work I do with leaders all over the globe, starts from the premise that we do not really know who we are, do not really understand how we affect others, and do not really grasp the daily and long-term consequences of our actions.

Hundreds of leadership books have been written in the last twenty years with the same fundamental message. If a manager or an executive treats his people with respect, earns their trust and acts with integrity, then loyalty and commitment will result and business objectives will be achieved. If that's true, and all those books have actually been read and not just boiled down to some self-congratulatory executive summary, how did we manage to find ourselves in such a big mess?

The problem is simple. Almost everyone believes in such a philosophy. But almost no one abides by it. And why should they? Every leader knows how easy it is to get away with bad behavior. As a result, most leaders eventually fail in the eyes of their followers. Today, expectations (not to mention hopes for inspiration), have never been lower. A new set of accountability standards must be put into place before followers will feel that it's safe to invest their commitment, passion, and loyalty in a leader again.

Becoming a leader worth following is difficult because the journey is so inadequately supported. Core values like integrity, trustworthiness, respect, and stewardship may gild corporate hallways and spice up motivational speeches, but no one really believes that they represent genuine living principles—not when self-interest is on the line. Anyone who works for a company today knows how self-interest gets rewarded, understands the pressure to self-aggrandize, recognizes that corruption has been made interpersonally legal. It's the rare and special leader who sheds those limitations on his way up the ladder to become someone truly worth following: A paragon of civility, a merchant of trust, a caretaker of those who depend on them for nurturance and direction.

Couldn't we use a few more such people today?

Who This Book Has Been Written For

This book is about that journey—the road to REAL leadership. It's not a smooth ride. In fact, for most people, the transformation requires a sharp turn off the path they have long been following. But the rewards of that journey are worth it. Specifically, this book has been written for three broad constituencies—rank and file employees, leadership development professionals, and leaders themselves—each of whom could use it to make their lives and worlds better. To that end, this book is intended as:

- ### A Dictionary and Thesaurus of Bad Leadership
  Bad leadership is something that all of us have experienced but few can articulate productively. For employees who are held hostage to bad leaders, I hope this book provides the vocabulary needed for articulating and surfacing those negative and destructive forces wherever they exist in an organization, thereby limiting their power and prompting much needed change. Use the terms that I use, ask the questions I pose, point out the behaviors I've exposed, and blame me if you have to, but let those Moron Managers know that what they are doing is not only unacceptable from a personal standpoint, but totally detrimental to the long-term success of your organization, as well. It's a fight worth winning. After all, it's your career, not to mention your matching 401K plan at stake. Ask the employees of Enron, OmniCom or Xerox (to name just a few) how that feels.

- **A Recalibration Instrument for REAL Leadership Development**

  The leadership development field has been using the same obsolete leadership model for at least the last 50 years—and look what it has produced. Future leaders have been selected and groomed, effectively, by looking in the rearview mirror. Technical skills, hard approaches, toughness, a killer instinct… little of that is functional any longer in a business world built on distance communication, entrepreneurship, networked relationships, flattened hierarchies, free agent workers, customer focus, innovative thinking, and frequent mergers and acquisitions. In order to be effective today, leaders need to be taught how to look inward, build new strengths and express a "softer" skill set in meaningful goal-oriented ways. Until that happens, every new generation of leader will continue to mimic outdated skills or stay off the playing field all together—diluting human capital, jeopardizing mergers, alienating customers and employees, and killing share prices. This book will help those in charge of leadership development programs recognize and promote REAL leadership in their organizations and build those core competencies for the future.

- **A Roadmap for Leaders Striving to Become Worth Following**

  For those already "in charge" or with leadership aspirations, I hope this book guides them in overcoming the challenges within—and using those challenges to their advantage. While we've all got the potential for REAL leadership, it's far, far easier to let that potential go to waste. Why? For starters, there's a conspiracy out there designed to bring out the worst in us. MBA programs get the ball rolling; corporate environments do more than their fair share to keep the process going strong. On top of that, self-awareness and interpersonal sensitivity is incredibly difficult for most people to master; these skills are unnatural and almost never taught in school or at the executive development retreat. Without a guide, the journey towards REAL leadership can be too difficult and its goals too elusive for most managers to have the stamina or interest to pursue. This book provides a real alternative to leadership development and expression, one that will leave its mark in the lives of those who embrace its message.

Whether you are a manager, a rank and file employee, or a participant in the great game of leadership development, I think you'll recognize some people in the pages that follow. Maybe you can do them a favor and pass them a well-marked copy of this book. They could sure use it... Someday, they might even thank you for it.

Who knows? Someday, you might even thank yourself...

Step 1

Getting REAL About Moron Management

Moron Manager (noun)

1. A relatively accomplished, hierarchically successful, but fundamentally undeserving recipient of superior status.

Moron Managing (verb)

1. To inflict greater work, heartache, or turmoil on reports and colleagues than necessary.

Moron Management (syndrome)

1. Symptoms include inflated sense of self-importance, misguided belief that others admire and choose to work for them, over-abundant but unearned sense of authority. Highly contagious at middle and senior ranks. Transmitted by predisposition toward ambition and lack of self-awareness.

Chapter One

····················

"Who Put That Moron In Charge?"
or
Why the Soft Stuff Is REAL-ly the Hard Stuff
(and Matters the Most)

The Journey to REAL Leadership
(And the bumps along the way)

"So… what kind of manager am I?"

"How do I affect the people around me?"

"Who do I need to become to bring out the best in others?"

Are you surprised that REAL leaders ask such questions of themselves all the time? Unlike most of us, they are not afraid to ask for directions. They know that introspection, critical self-examination, painful honesty, and a willingness to change and grow are essential leadership tools. They understand that "becoming a leader worth following" is not a destination with a comfortable resting spot to gaze down upon the world from, but a journey with no rest along the way.

This book is about that journey. The path has been traveled by others before, but your experience of it will depend very much on how far you are willing to go. Though I can promise you that your journey will be rewarding, fulfilling, meaningful and extremely worthwhile, I can also assure you that it will not feel natural or easy along the way. Perhaps that's why so few of us have experienced REAL leadership first hand.

What do I mean by REAL leadership? To make it easier to picture, I've even developed a nifty acronym. Without fail, such rare individuals are:

> **R**esponsible (for themselves and others)
> **E**mpowering (of themselves and others)
> **A**ccountable (for themselves and others)
> **L**oving (to themselves and others)

It may sound simple but it's not. In fact, it may be the hardest thing you'll ever do. But before we get to all that, let's start with a little story—the journey one manager made towards REAL leadership.

Like all good stories it has its share of surprising turns—some scary, some inspirational, some downright touching. Despite a tough beginning, you'll be glad to know the story has a happy ending—this time.

Being Frank: A Self-Love Story

Frank was a vice president and general manager at TRW, in charge of one of their credit operations. Like any tough, no-nonsense manager, he ran a tight ship. His department was doing well. His employees were meeting their performance goals. Then, in a blow that Frank utterly failed to see coming, three of his top people resigned within the same week. The reason? They'd simply had enough of him.

I was called in to help determine what had happened. Specifically, I was asked to figure out how Frank's role as leader of a vital profit-center had so suddenly been called into question and whether it was even worth it for the company to keep him around any longer. Luckily for me, I was able to interview Frank's three key people before they actually left the company. Through them and through others who remained inside Frank's domain, I learned a lot about Frank's leadership style.

Despite Frank's success as a manager, it turned out that he was actually despised by the people who worked for him. Why? Well, for starters, he was abusive and threatening. He ordered people around, treated them with disdain, and regularly insinuated that he could derail their careers if they didn't kowtow to him. As a result, his employees came to see him as dangerous and they developed all sorts of elaborate schemes for keeping him out of their work and lives. The fact that three key people had left Frank was just the tip of the iceberg. As I dug deeper, I learned that Frank's management style was causing problems even outside his core group. Other departments had become resistant to cooperating with him. Even his peers, people who were under no direct threat from him, were embarrassed by his management approach. He threw his weight around like an arrogant and demanding dictator.

At first, when I shared all of this feedback with Frank, he didn't believe a word. But he was faced with a set of undeniable facts. His key people had left him, his peers were avoiding him, and he was on the brink of being fired. When that reality sank in, he was speechless. His abrasive and arrogant front crumbled like a cliff-face in an avalanche. Together, we decided to do something about his problem. I told him that he could change how he managed by changing who he was—in a deep and meaningful way. I told him that the journey would be very hard and that there would be many bumps along the way. I also told him not to underestimate how much work he would have to do, and would have to keep doing, to become a leader that others would want to follow. And I told him that in the end, the payoff, as measured in personal life and career satisfaction, would make that hard work very worthwhile doing. Given the alternative, it's not as if Frank had much choice. With his full commitment, we set forth together.

Are you curious whether our hero managed to pull off his transformation? Or could you care less because Frank seems like such a bad guy? Before you settle too comfortably into a harsh evaluation of poor Frank, let me put his circumstances into a broader context. Despite how it may sound, Frank was not an unusually bad manager. Nor was he a deliberately hurtful person. Few Moron Managers are. Hardly any of them drive into work in the morning thinking:

> *How can I alienate, discourage, disempower, and disenfranchise my key people today? What approach should I use to get the least out of them while laying the blame for my failure at their feet? Where, in the fertile soil of my management behavior, should I plant the seeds of my own eventual demise?*

But that's what an awful lot of managers end up doing, at all levels, at organizations all around the world. Typically, it's not a sin of malice or willful destruction. If anything, it's almost always a sin that arises out of neglect, insecurity, insensitivity, lack of self-awareness, lack of empathy, fear of failure, fear of the truth, and a push for speed at all costs. Nevertheless, whether intended or not, such an approach to leadership extracts a terribly high price, in the short-term and the long-term, in organizations everywhere. We could all do, and become, so much more, if only we knew how. By the end of this book, I hope that you'll believe me and take the steps necessary to change your corner of the world, as well.

As for our hero, over time, he made some fundamental changes in the way he operated. Doing so opened up his relationships at work and created a world he had not imagined possible: An environment where communication, teamwork, productivity and innovation sprang from mutual respect, generosity of spirit, teaching, learning, striving and sharing—without duplicity, falseness, manipulation, or greed. How did he come to arrive in this brave new world? Ironically, much of Frank's progress came through the help of those very same employees he had been treating so badly. Frank learned how to meet with his people—on a regular basis—and ask them how THEY thought he could become a better leader. He learned how to talk to his family about what he could do differently with them, too. And he learned how to ask himself the same kinds of deep and critical questions. Through this well-rounded self-examination, he explored his most basic assumptions and came to terms with the aspects of himself that needed to change. He gained clarity about his values, the things he really believed in, and learned how to use those values as both a starting point and an end goal in his journey. Was he making any progress towards REAL leadership? To evaluate that, he learned how to objectively contrast how he was perceived by others with how he wanted to be perceived, a measurement of the difference between his intentions and his actions. Some days, the verdict was encouraging. Other days, he realized just how far he still had to go.

Gradually, he began to change how he acted around the office and at home. It felt very awkward at first, and it was something he had to work hard at—all the time. In order to make his changes real, he committed to a different goal each day. On one day, for example, he declared, "I will praise three people before five o'clock." On another day, he said, "I will ask for someone's honest opinion this morning and actually use what I learn from them before the week is out." On still another day, he promised himself, "I will meet with two people to find out how I came across to them this month; and I will change my behavior tomorrow based on what I learn." Little by little, the changes set in. Eventually, they even began to feel natural. Making it real transformed him as a leader.

How did those internal changes impact the world outside him? The truth is, in the first month, Frank didn't feel as if anything outside of himself had changed. But then he noticed that there was a drastic difference in the people around him. He became aware that his people now wanted him to succeed instead of fail. The change was most apparent in their work. They were giving their best efforts now, working with him, instead of against him, because doing so gave them so much back in return. Before they had talked about team spirit but didn't really mean it; now they worked together as a team because it was natural and fulfilling. At the end of three months, Frank took another step forward. He was able to successfully re-recruit two of the three key people who had left him in the first place. And within eighteen months, Frank went on to become division president. He knew that this accomplishment had much less to do with him than the people around him. He had not crawled up another rung on the ladder by himself; his people had pushed him up because they respected and cared for him as a leader. He was grateful to them for that; and he promised not to forget what he had learned. He knew that being a leader would not get any easier. Every day he caught himself falling back into his old comfort zone. The tendency to revert was always around the corner. But he could see how his hard work to become a REAL leader was paying off in all aspects of his life. Knowing how far he had come gave him the commitment to keep going even further.

I was proud of Frank and, believe it or not, his people were, too. We all recognized that it's incredibly hard for a person in a position of power to make a commitment to grow and change and actually follow through on it. Imagine doing it yourself some time, and you'll see what I mean. Maybe, by the end of this book, you'll know what it feels like through personal experience, not just imagination. I think the payoff you'll discover through that process will make you grateful for the journey and even all the bumps along the way.

Becoming Less Right
(A forewarning)

As you can see through Frank's story, it's not easy becoming a REAL leader. And since it's not easy, this book, by its very nature, presents a rather significant difficulty. What difficulty is that, you ask? Well, the things I have to say in it—and more specifically, the things I have to say about you, your colleagues, your boss, and your organization—are very, very hard.

Will it be hard every step of the way? Pretty much. Though some times it will be kind of funny and some times it will be kind of sad. Your reaction—including your denial, your delight, your disbelief, and your deep anger—will depend on how close to the bone, at any particular moment, my message hits you. After all, it was Aristotle who said that the only difference between comedy and tragedy is distance. He claimed that when we see the difficulties and problems of someone's life from far away, we get a good laugh. But when we see them up close, especially when we imagine that those problems and difficulties are actually our own, we cry. Either way, like I said to Frank, fasten your seatbelt because it's going to be a helluva ride. But that doesn't mean the journey won't be worth taking.

Most leadership books are designed to make you feel wonderful. Which is nice. And maybe even worth the price. But probably not going to give you much insight into the REAL challenges of leadership. Instead, they put a bandage on your critical injuries, pat you on the back, send you home, and sell a lot of copies in the process.

This book, in contrast, is going to take courage to read. But that's okay because courage is something you'll be learning a lot about along the way. In fact, by the end of this book you will come to embrace a model of leadership in which Courage is front and center, flanked on either wing by Passion and Irreverence. For example, in this book and in your leadership journey, you will need to be passionate about a lot of things, including your need to change. You will also need to be courageous about a lot of things, including your need to look at yourself in the mirror. And you will need to be irreverent about a lot of things, including the traits and skills you currently consider to be vital to your character and your management career.

As they say at the gym, and in the gestalt therapy centers: NO PAIN, NO GAIN. Anything worth doing—let alone, anything worth becoming—comes at a price.

Courage, passion, irreverence. It takes all three to learn how to really examine your assumptions, to accurately perceive how you come across in the world, and to discover what you need to change to become something better. So many leadership books are about confirming what you already know to be true. In many ways, this leadership book is about proving you have so much left to learn. It's not about becoming more certain. If anything, it's about becoming less right.

A Moron Manager's Biggest Strength
(Is their biggest weakness)

My biggest problem in explaining all of this, however, is also your biggest problem in understanding what I mean. My problem is that the best way to understand REAL leadership is to look very closely at its opposite form, the subspecies known as Moron Manager. Why is that, you ask? Surely, you insist, it's more appealing to admire the good than it is to stare at the bad? I agree, but unfortunately, REAL leadership, like certain exquisite and beautiful butterflies, is very rare. We have a tendency, when we are lucky enough to encounter it, to think of it in lofty and unrealistic terms—failing utterly to see the blood, sweat, and tears that goes into making it REAL. The best way to understand what it actually takes to be a REAL leader is to see how far a Moron Manager has to go in order to become one. And that's not always a pretty sight.

Don't believe me that real leadership is rare? Well, try to recall some of the real leaders you've worked with over the years. Does anyone come to mind? Anyone? Okay, so let's flip that around instead. Think of all the Moron Managers you've ever known. Remember how they:

- Set goals and then did nothing to help you achieve them?
- Told you that their door was always open but never listened to what you had to say?
- Blamed your performance for their lousy numbers?
- Gave you feedback that felt less like an insightful reading of your strengths and weaknesses than a Rorschach Test of their management failures?

Yup, those Moron Managers. Self-serving, self-aggrandizing, insecure, evasive.

Still having trouble picturing anyone in particular? Well, try this visualization exercise. Imagine:

Your own
BOSS*

★ **B**ullying
  Opportunistic
  Self-serving
  Short-sighted

Quick! Turn the page!

Sorry! I didn't mean the BOSS you currently have. No, not the one who's looking over your shoulder right now while you're reading this book. But some BOSS, sometime, somewhere, at that other company perhaps, the one you left to come here, where everything is perfect, just like paradise…

Yeah, *that* BOSS. Remember how it went with [*insert name here*]? But you got even didn't you? Does any of this sound familiar? Remember how you:

- Said "yes" to their ideas, showed interest in their visionary plans, laughed at their jokes, suffered their bad moods, and unreasonable demands cheerfully… *but really couldn't stand them!*

Or, how you…

- Took on projects with an air of eagerness, commitment and drive but didn't accomplish those goals and performed way below your abilities… *because you could have cared less if they succeeded and knew that they would take all the credit anyway!*

Or, how you…

- Put up with their lack of attention, their miserliness with their time, their general bad manners, and their personal indifference… *and then told them you were leaving for the money when you jumped ship to a competitor!*

Or, how you…

- Pretended that they were important, exciting, interesting, and wonderful to be around… *but forgot they even existed outside the office!*

It's true, isn't it? You've been through a lot. I hope that in some small way this book helps you heal those scars—even a little. But if you want more salve for your wounds, or just a good laugh, read on...

Because it's even funnier how Moron Managers view themselves. Over the years, I've had the dubious pleasure of interviewing thousands of them all over the world. In the early days, I would just innocently pose a few simple questions and listen. One of the questions I always asked in one form or another was this:

"What's your greatest strength as a manager?"
"What do you pride yourself on?"
"What makes you so very good at what you do?"

I was amazed by the answers, not because they were so varied or profound or loaded with insight but because they were always the same. They were even phrased the same way, from manager to manager, up and down the corporate ladder, across industries, no matter the country, region, or market. My greatest asset? Oh, well it's definitely:

"My ability to deal with people"

Are you still laughing? Be careful, someone's going to suspect you've gone off the deep end. But if you're having troubles getting that gut-splitter under control, then just think about poor me. The words themselves never fail to send a chill down my spine. Reading a statement like that in black and white makes two things clear: First, that Moron Managers view their work relationships as something that requires an "ability," as if "people skills" were a chapter in some corporate training manual. And second, that they view "people" in general as something to be "dealt" with.

I don't know about you, but when I think about the word "deal," lots of stuff come to mind—problems, headaches, issues, setbacks—but none of that is about building relationships or genuinely helping others surpass themselves, let alone about being "REAL."

The Flip Side of Dealing with People
(Nobody likes to be "dealt with.")

Then I would have the privilege of interviewing that Moron Manager's subordinates. Ah, what an anticipated pleasure that was! To find out what someone really thinks about their BOSS! You might expect, however, that most employees would be a little reserved about snitching on their manager, that they would hold back their true, uncensored feelings from an outsider. Not a chance. Door closed, official "listener" at hand, tape recorder button pushed on, the truth poured out as readily as if the punch had been spiked at the year-end holiday party.

Like their managers, I asked subordinates the same question except in mirror-image form:

"What kind of liabilities do you see in your manager?"
"What kinds of weaknesses or problems does your
manager present to you?"
"Where does your manager fall short?"

And those answers, too—at least the immediate, short-version, printable-in-a-book-that-children-might-read answers—were remarkably the same:

"The way they deal with people"

More stuff would come out. Just for kicks let's include some of it here:

"My manager is unclear about direction."

"My manager says one thing and does another."

"My manager does not value my input."

"My manager treats me like dirt."

"My manager is self-serving."

"My manager is inaccessible."

"My manager gives me no feedback about how I'm doing."

"My manager is rude and unreasonable."

"My manager demands things of me he doesn't expect of himself."

"My manager is _____."

"My manager is _____."

The blank ones at the bottom are for you. Pretend we've just closed the door and I've asked you what you really think about your own BOSS. Don't be shy, they aren't around. Add your own favorites to the list. It's fun just thinking about, don't you agree? Hey, we all know what it's like. We've all got bosses. They're really something, aren't they!

Since you're enjoying yourself so much, I won't even bring up the fact that the comments you just made about those Moron Managers are probably the same things that someone else would make about you. I'm not sure you've got the irreverence for that yet, let alone the courage and passion. So we'll save the truth of that little reciprocal nightmare for later.

Hang in there, you'll make it.

So, What the Heck Are Managers Good at? (And why does that make them morons?)

Could all those managers really be that inept, callous, confused, and misguided? Shouldn't the fact that they were the cream of the crop, the top of the heap, extremely successful by all traditional measures, mean something? After all, they'd risen through the ranks the hard way, learning the ropes, making the grade, earning the big bucks, distinguishing themselves from their colleagues in the process—so what in the world was going on?

During all the interviews I conducted, I could count on one hand the number of times a subordinate told me that his manager was not very smart. Similarly, I was never told that a manager lacked an understanding of the technical aspects of the job. In fact, I almost never heard that a manager had any shortcoming whatsoever in an area that could be described as requiring a "real ability," a "concrete skill," a "core-competency," or however else we describe what it is that leadership types are supposed to possess to be effective.

Yet, the evidence was stunning. By all objective standards, the overwhelming majority SUCKED at being managers.

Now, don't get me wrong. It's not as if what those managers did for a living wasn't complex. In fact, their jobs required relatively rare and certainly demanding technical skills. Developing budgets. Laying out strategies. Designing work systems. Figuring out supply chain needs. Forecasting sales projections. It was all downright intimidating.

The question for me therefore became: At what aspect of management did they suck? And, even more importantly, why was this fact obscured to everyone involved (including the higher-ups who made the promotions; the Moron Managers, themselves, who thought they were top-notch; and—to some degree—the subordinates who had given their managers a relatively free pass by not rising up and rebelling in frustration, indignation, and outrage)?

Ask subordinates what a manager is good at and you hear nothing but the technical skills. Delve into where a manager fails miserably and you will get a litany of interpersonal disasters. In common parlance, we refer to the human side of managing versus the rational, logical, and concrete side as the difference between the "soft stuff" and the "hard stuff." Managers know the soft stuff is important, after all they say that what they are best at is their "ability to deal with people." Subordinates just happen to disagree—with all their hearts.

Confusing enough? Do you like to listen to the sound of one hand clapping? Are you enjoying all the paradoxes in this book so far? Because here comes another one... and it's one of the biggest of all:

Almost every manager gets to where they are because of the hard stuff, their technical skills...

But almost every manager thinks they got there because of the soft stuff, their interpersonal skills...

Could it be that the soft stuff is really hard?

The Technical Skills
(So hard, they're really soft.)

Daniel Goleman, best-selling author of *Emotional Intelligence*, calls the technical skills a ticket to entry. Managers build them the hard way, climbing the ranks and practicing on the job, through years of education, training, and "development." Little by little, they accumulate this experience—a hardcore knowledge and understanding of what is required by those below them to do their jobs well. Although Moron Managers may not acknowledge it, believe me, they're grateful for those skills. In fact, most of them are so grateful that they find them impossible to let go of... but more on that problem later.

One reason we call the technical skills the "hard stuff" is because we work hard to learn them. (Another reason is because they are "hard-edged," but more on that later, too.) You don't wake up one day and understand how to design a bridge, operate a computer, fly a plane, or develop a national marketing campaign. You wouldn't expect a high school graduate with the best chemistry score to be given the directorship of a drug company's research laboratory. She'd have to earn her way to that position, taking the right courses in college and graduate school, distinguishing herself in her own research, showing the innovation, initiative, and ability to truly make a mark on the company's new products. But even if she did all that, when she finally achieved the position of director, she'd still fail at leadership; I can almost guarantee it.

Huh?

Look at it this way. When you're a lab tech, your job isn't interpersonal at all because you're interacting with equipment. When you're a supervisor in that same lab, you're responsible for four people and you report to one. When you're a manager of the department, you've got eight supervisors and 20 techs below that and a few regional bosses above. When you're the leader of a global pharmaceutical company, you might have 50,000 people matrixed into you in one way or another.

Along the way, the percentage of the job that was technical in nature decreased and the percentage that was interpersonal went up dramatically. Why? Well, you now have people—your people—to do the jobs that used to be yours. If you're a good manager, you're okay with that. Heck, you want them to be even better than you ever were.

But if you're feeling stressed out and overworked managing those below you, then you're like most managers—you're having significant difficulty letting go of those technical skills you once knew and loved. Or, as William Onken, the noted time management expert once quipped: "If you are doing the work of two people, the chances are that one of them reports to you." But that's not their fault, it's yours.

Think of the nature of the day-to-day interactions involved. Supervisors tend to be single location, staring over the shoulder of the one being supervised, literally leading that person through the motions of the job. Supervisors need to be skilled at the technical aspects of the job they are supervising. It goes with the territory. But they also need to have other soft qualities, too, although these are not as critical. Managers tend to be multi-locational, even global, managing from a distance rather than from visible proximity. Here, even softer skills need to come to the forefront in order to be effective. CEOs may never know or talk to—may never even meet—the many, many thousands of people who rely on them for leadership. In other words, the higher up the ladder you go, the greater the increase in the sheer numbers of people who come to depend on your direction. Which means that the higher up the ladder you go, the less useful your technical skills are and the more critical your interpersonal skills. Which means the higher up the ladder you go, the more likely you are to run into significant interpersonal and leadership troubles instead of technical ones.

What happens to those technical skills? Why do they stop being important?

Take an auditor at one of the Big Five accounting firms. (Big Three? Big Two and a Half? Let's not even go there.) Certain qualities will make that auditor successful in his first few jobs: Attention to detail, precision, inability to be easily influenced, narrow focus, personal alacrity, a certain dogged persistence about impersonal things.

Now, send that auditor a few rungs up the management ladder. Those very qualities that made him so good as a functional contributor probably will prevent or derail him in any kind of supervisory role. Similarly, if you take the things that make a supervisor really good at what they do, oftentimes those are the very same things that prevent them from being an effective manager. The very skills that made you successful as a manager, prevent you from being an effective leader. In fact, in order to have any chance at all of success in leadership every Moron Manager needs to relax their grip on technical skills, the things that got them in the door. They need to loosen their grasp on them altogether, say goodbye, and let them go.

But it sure isn't easy to do, and that's only the beginning of becoming someone who leads a group, instead of someone who runs one.

The problem is, no one teaches interpersonal skills to those who find themselves in management, nor are they even valued in people who somehow obtain them on their own. Don't believe me? Well, have you ever seen a merit badge for human decency or team play? No? Take a look at school course lists. See anything on interpersonal skills? Not a chance. How about corporate training and development programs? Anything there on building respect or generating trust? Didn't think so.

Engineers know what it's like. When they graduate and get that first real-life project management posting, they stare reality in the face for the first time and promptly receive a cold, hard slap:

"What you learned sitting in the classroom does not apply here. You're going to have to figure out what really matters in order to survive."

Business schools are the worst. All that time spent on case studies, financial analysis, strategic design, and Power Point presentations may as well have been spent studying deep sea life forms. Sure the diploma looks nice. That's why they hired you. Now, go hang it on the wall behind your desk and get to work.

By the time a poor manager has figured out that their real job is leading people, they've already become a first class Moron. And no one's going to change them now, not if they can help it. That would mean admitting a lot of things that would be painful, humbling, shocking, and perhaps even humiliating. They certainly don't prepare anyone for that in B-School.

But, if the Soft Stuff is so important (and managers seem to acknowledge this in some weird way by claiming it as their chief attribute or strength), why do we denigrate it as "soft"? Why do we pooh-pooh it as wimpy and weak when it really takes incredible strength? Why, even if we acknowledge that it's vital at some level, do we assume that it's an innate skill, bequeathed through genes, and not important enough to be worked on directly, deliberately, and vigorously?

Try asking any manager whether they'd prefer to be treated with the Soft Stuff or the Hard Stuff. Chances are they'll say that all they want is to be managed fairly, by which they mean respectfully, caringly, sensitively, empathetically, and compassionately. If you asked them, "Well, why don't you treat your own people like that," they'll dismiss that approach as soft, squishy, touchy-feely, and "un-leaderly." After all, as managers, they have to be tough, hard-nosed, hard-edged, and no-nonsense.

Acting tough and being hard is simply a justification for managers to be mean and an excuse for them to be lazy about the work necessary to be soft. The truth is, Moron Managers make management hard because they are really soft in a different sense—they lack the fortitude, strength and courage to learn any differently. They're ill-equipped to get to where they really need to be: A place of immense vulnerability and terrific personal strength. They're too scared. It would mean putting themselves on the line, trusting others, caring enough to care what they think, and being compassionate, and self-aware.

A leader, on the other hand, takes the risks necessary to be as soft as hard can be. That's a difference that I hope will become very clear before too long.

It's a Mad Mad Mad Mad World
(The self-perpetuating moron manager machine)

It's not as if the phenomenon of the Moron Manager is something we've just stumbled upon. No, I'm afraid it's been around for a very long time. Listen to this example and see if it sounds familiar.

In the 1300s, the Spanish and British Empires sent out huge ships to explore the known world and snatch unclaimed territory for themselves. These ships sailed for three or four whole years at a time ushering in a new era for "enlightened civilization." The problem was the fleet commanders noticed that huge numbers of their crew were dying from terrible diseases, such as beriberi and scurvy. The British figured out around that time that the way to address most of these diseases was fairly simple—include citrus fruits, with their large doses of vitamin C, as part of daily nutrition. This gave them a tremendous advantage over the Spanish by keeping "their people" alive!

Yet, amazingly, it wasn't until the 1600s that citrus fruit was mandatory on all British fishing vessels.

In other words, human beings have an incredible, nearly boundless capacity for cruelty and a deep apathy to the needs of their fellow human beings. And, if the managers of the British fleet are any indication, it doesn't matter how many lives are lost in the process of being "consistent" with policies, traditions and practices—they're going to go ahead anyway. Think about that the next time you visit your company's supply room and notice the conspicuous absence of any crates of grapefruit!

What a mess. Don't you agree? But how real a problem is it? Well, consider the wide range of impact within succession planning, hiring, and CEO selection.

By the time a manager has gotten to the middle ranks, the probability that he will be fired for some kind of technical or intellectual flaw is virtually non-existent. The probability that they will be fired because they're interpersonal failures, however, is incredibly high.

Jeff Christian, a colleague and the CEO of a prominent executive search firm, knows what I mean. He puts it this way:

"People are hired for experience and fired for personality."

We know this is true. We only need to think about the Moron Managers we've seen get canned over the years. But the inanity of the situation runs deep. When we interview or promote, we make our decisions based on one set of criteria—experience and technical skills—even when we KNOW we're going to evaluate success (or lack thereof) based on an entirely different set of criteria—interpersonal skills, leadership dynamism, team-orientation, or other "soft stuff."

Even at the CEO level, when you examine the revolving door that is the condition of corporate leadership these days, personality is the underlying reason why people get replaced. The analysts or the board of directors or the Wall Street Journal might say that it's because the CEO didn't meet the numbers, but that is a shallow explanation of what really happened. The reason why the CEO didn't meet the numbers was because they weren't able to energize an audience of committed employees who could help work towards a vision. They weren't leaders because they had no followers. Though they may have created plenty of enemies…

Isn't it all kind of nuts? It's like the very functioning of an organization's "People Systems" produces Moron Managers as some kind of industrial waste by-product! As for the poor Moron Managers themselves, it almost makes you feel sorry for them, doesn't it? Nah, I know what you're really thinking. You still want to see that they get what's coming to them.

Don't worry, you will.

The Royal Road To Getting REAL
* Redefining What Matters *

- ### "Your people" are not a deck of cards. So don't DEAL with them, LEAD them.

  Moron Managers view their people as pieces in a puzzle or tools for achieving group (or their own selfish) objectives. This bias impedes managerial-associate relationships. Your people really respond to being treated like human beings. Imagine that!

- ### The SOFT STUFF is really hard, but matters most.

  Interpersonal authenticity is more important than anything else in becoming a leader worth following. But no one tells us that interpersonal skills are key, let alone teaches us how to develop them. By assuming that we are effective in those areas, we underestimate how deficient we actually are and how hard we need to work to improve.

- ### What you learned on the way up is what you need to forget once you arrive.

  Technical skills get us further up the career ladder but do nothing to help us become better leaders. In fact, our appreciation for our technical skills gets in the way when we assume a leadership position. We think we can do our subordinate's job better than he can and fail to provide them with the support and guidance they really need.

....

Chapter Two

Just Deserts

or

How a Moron Manager Inflates, Suppresses & Denies Their Way into Career & Life Derailment

Let's suppose you have a friend you really care about—and you know that friend is a Moron Manager. Having read this book, you can see that your friend's management career is headed for trouble. You'd like to help them avoid a painful fate. Even more importantly, you'd like to see them grow and change in order to become a leader worth following—someone who affects the people around them in a deeply positive way, who makes a unique mark on the world and who accomplishes significant things, big or small, every day. How do you help your friend get off the path he is on and get on to the path towards REAL leadership?

The most difficult part of enlightening someone about their Moron Manager behavior is that they inevitably will refuse to believe a single word you say. No one ever actually sees themselves as a BOSS. In fact, we all want to see ourselves as being better than we actually are. That tendency leads to some amazing delusions. Take this real life story as an illustration:

> *Linda J. Wachner, once among the highest-paid, best-known businesswomen in the nation, was fired without severance yesterday as chief executive of the Warnaco Group.*
>
> *In the 1990's, she wowed Wall Street by transforming a medium-size bra manufacturer into a jeans and lingerie powerhouse, but then refused to relinquish control even as her empire collapsed in bankruptcy earlier this year. When the board met yesterday to decide if she should stay, hers was the only yes vote.*
>
> *A hard-charging boss who spewed obscenities, Ms. Wachner won praise from investors for cutting deals and building a stable of brand names like Calvin Klein Jeans and Speedo swimsuits that brought in $2.25 billion a year in sales at its peak. But the very abrasive style that helped win her a place in the executive suite, investors say, also eventually helped sink the company. She alienated talent-*

ed staff and an important business partner, Calvin Klein, who sued her and called her "vile." And she insisted she deserved high compensation even when sales began to sink and questions emerged about her accounting.

In an interview yesterday, Ms. Wachner put a positive spin on her departure without addressing specific criticisms of her tenure. "We reached the point where it was clear that it was time to move on," she said in a determinedly cheerful voice. "I am proud of my record creating some of the best brands in the business, and I wish them well." (New York Times, November 16, 2001)

And, we wish Linda well, too. It's going to be a cold, cold world out there now that she doesn't have her loyal followers around to keep her warm. And no severance package either! Do the injustices ever stop? Although, a compensation expert who analyzed Linda's earnings in recent years assures us that she'll be able to make it somehow. "At the end of the day she is worth more than the company," we're told. That's good because the company itself went bankrupt—a choice they made because it was the only way to avoid having to pay Linda four times what the organization was worth!

Let's take a closer look at how Linda's weaknesses—as described by the article—contributed to her and her company's demise.

According to the *New York Times*, Linda:

- Was hard-charging and spewed obscenities. (Not to be judgmental, but that doesn't sound like a lot of fun to be around.)
- Had an abrasive style that alienated her people. (Remember, one of her most important strategic partners called her "vile.")
- Did not take any personal responsibility for the company's sharp decrease in sales. (Though she was probably happy to accept the

credit Wall Street gave her when those sales initially increased.)
- Was completely oblivious to the damage she did to her followers and her organization. (Or was she just being sensitive to her own motivational needs by insisting that her compensation be unaffected by her performance?)
- Remains seemingly unrepentant, unabashed, and impervious to any feeling of guilt or blame about the way she left her organization. ("I am proud of my record... I wish them well.")

Sound extreme? I wish that it were. But to get an idea of how different that picture could be, try this on for size:

Moron Managers...	REAL Leaders...
Are self-aggrandizing and self-promoting	Are humble and self-effacing
Take all the credit and share all the blame	Take all the blame and share all the credit
Think in terms of daily gains and losses—primarily financial	Think in terms of long-term impact—primarily personal and interpersonal
Service their own needs first and make others an afterthought	Services others first and in return are well-served
Think that power is a limited resource that they have to gain the most of	See influence as an unlimited resource that they have to give away

Kind of puts it in perspective, doesn't it? Ah, the Moron Manager. Delusional without foundation, absurdly narcissistic, self-righteous, and self-serving. Yup, it's pretty ugly stuff. Like Linda J. Wachner, Moron Managers self-aggrandize, self-promote, and self-protect because they view these behaviors as the necessary foundation for their career development and progression. Given a choice between maximizing short-term gains and doing what's right, Moron Managers always maximize short-term gains. Given a choice between treating subordinates respectfully and treating them like dirt, Moron Managers actually think that they are doing their jobs well by being as "hard" and "tough" on the people around them as possible.

But surely, Linda's obliviousness is rare, you insist. How could she not see the effect she was having on others?

One of the fun things about Moron Managers is how incurably blind they are to their own failings and faults. They've long ago stopped asking *why* they do the things that they do; and they have stopped reflecting on or even thinking about how *what* they do affects the people around them. The fact that those two things together are where managers spend all their time—and what management, and certainly "leadership" is supposedly all about—is an irony that completely escapes them.

Instead of introspection, Moron Managers allow themselves the gift of baseless and unbridled self-confidence, and the free pass of blamelessness. They are secure in what they do and never at fault for the way others feel.

How do we know this? Just ask. When things go wrong between a Moron Manager and his employees (as they usually do) the Moron Manager will blame everyone and everything except themselves. If you want specifics, ask them why an employee under performed, dropped out emotionally or packed up and left for another job. The Moron Manager will say it is because they were not up to the task or folded under pressure or ran to the competition for more money or to another division because it was softer or easier. You could try asking the employee the true reason, but you won't get a straight answer—they've tried that already and probably have gotten slapped down for doing so.

Remember the difference between comedy and tragedy? Depending on your point of view, the sad or funny thing about a Moron Manager is that they always get their just deserts. Somewhere along the line, they plant the seeds of their own destruction.

Care to see how that comes about?

Lies My Moron Manager Told Me
(How moron managers fool themselves... and reveal their true nature.)

All Moron Managers engage in certain self-deluding behaviors that eventually trip them up. I call those behaviors Inflation, Suppression, and Denial—but you can call them lying, avoiding the truth, and shifting the blame. Together, they constitute a first-class ticket on a fast train headed towards career and life derailment. If you or anyone you care about has got a seat on that train, this would be a very good time to start making other travel plans.

INFLATION

Sure, you're a six handicap.
Today was just the exception.

Inflation is such a common Moron Management technique that we generally take it for granted. It's the standard way managers primp themselves up despite the lie. Corporations do it all the time. Just check their annual reports. If the numbers were good that year, it's not because the markets were up and a rising tide raises all boats, it's because "we have the best damn executive team going!" On the other hand, if the numbers were lousy, you can be sure that same executive team is blameless. Instead, the fault always lies in the external things: The market contracted or the new competition rode into town and clouded the air. In short, inflation allows the company, and the people in it, to think and act as if it is better than it actually is and protect itself from the consequences of failure. So it goes with managers, who generally inflate themselves around things which no one has ever taught them how to do well.

Here's one example: Try asking a Moron Manager how honest they are. No, don't tell me what they say. I already know the answer. They will be quick to confess that they are exceedingly honest. (It's probably one of their weak points, all this honesty. If only they could be more political and conniving!) About 95% of CEOs say the same thing. However, a survey which asked their secretaries, "Has your boss ever asked you to lie?" produced the same percentage. "Absolutely. On a regular basis," they said. Some of those lies were simple things such as, "Tell them I'm in a meeting." Or, "Don't submit this report." But it also crossed the line into more serious matters such as, "Destroy this document." Or, "Tell my wife I had to leave town for the afternoon."

Recognize any of those behaviors in the Moron Managers you know? Of course, we know it's not their fault. They're not inherently dishonest. They're just dishonest depending on the situation. Their intentions are good. They wouldn't lie if they didn't have to lie. But instead of answering that they are basically dishonest people (the truth as seen in their actions), they cling to the ideal of themselves (the truth of their intentions) and rely on excuses to inflate their honesty to sanctified levels. Too bad no one in the hallway will ever say, "There goes Bob, the most honest manager here."

It's the same with a manager's ability at managing. Witness the question raised in the previous chapter. When asked what made them the success they are today, most managers answered, "My ability to deal with people." The good news is that this represents a very strong reservoir of high self-esteem. The bad news is that it's completely unfounded. We know it's not true. We just have to ask subordinates what their manager's greatest weakness is, and those subordinates invariably will reply, "Their ability to deal with people." So why the self-deception? Why the irrational inflation of such an important and meaningful ability in spite of, some might say in dispute of, such weakness and failing?

It's different with leaders. The great leaders I've interviewed are constantly vigilant about their people and how what they do affects them. They are *never* good enough. They know that "managing people" is something they are always going to have to work on improving. I don't recall, on the other hand, a single Moron Manager who answered that they were actually worried about their people skills. Instead, they exaggerate how well they interact with their subordinates and overestimate how well those same people think of them in return.

As far as climbing to the summit goes, that makes "people skills" not exactly terra firma. Mention that to a Moron Manager the next time you see them feeling around for a good grip on the next rung of the corporate ladder. If you listen closely, you might even be able to hear their screams as they plummet into the chasm below.

SUPPRESSION

Block. Ignore. Repeat.
Block. Ignore. Repeat.

Most of us are familiar with the term repression, the psychological mechanism which unconsciously pushes painful or inflammatory knowledge someplace deep where we don't have to think about it directly. It's not without cost, however. We pay a price.

Suppression is different. Suppression is an active act. It's taking information that can't possibly be interpreted any other way and giving ourselves a free pass just the same.

Through suppression, a Moron Manager consciously repackages the facts of what's actually going on in order to avoid thinking about the harsh consequences of reality. It's the way they justify their hurtful actions. When one Moron Manager I know told his subordinate the cold hard "truth" about her performance on the job and she ran from the room weeping, he didn't question his approach or his motivations or even his communication style. Instead, suppression allowed him to say to a colleague later on, "she got a little teary-eyed," and he felt all better about himself without having to change a thing.

I once had another Moron Manager client who was having considerable difficulty working with his division. No matter how much I tried to talk with him about what was going on, he completely resisted my efforts to open up about the facts. So, naturally, I interviewed his secretary hoping for some real insight. She told me that she was his fourth executive assistant in five months and, after only a little prodding, implied that he was abusive. When I went back to my client and innocently asked him about why all his previous secretaries had left, he had the most amazing explanations for each and every one, none of which had anything to do with him. I really was impressed. Here was someone who would go far—if only that could be achieved by lying shamelessly about the consequences of his actions. My client was able to suppress the clear message that people did not want to work with him or for him by repackaging that information in such a way that made their leaving appear to be their choice instead of his responsibility.

The REAL leaders I know are not merely sensitive to the impressions and perceptions of others; they actively seek those perceptions out, probing for more even when it is painful information for them to hear. Why? Because they know that it is the only way they are going to get the feedback they need to grow and change as the demands of their leadership trust requires.

Moron Managers, on the other hand, push away unpleasant information even when confronted directly by the truth. Sure, it makes the day easier to get through, but a price gets paid. The manager loses the opportunity for growth by ignoring the call for self-reflection and self-examination. The question shouldn't be, "What's their problem?" It ought to be, "What did I do that I could have or should have done differently?" How else are we going to learn the truth?

DENIAL

It's not just a river in Egypt.

Denial allows a Moron Manager to avoid the pain they need to feel in order to grow. It buffers them from the feelings of anxiety and inadequacy that they actually need to build from to become REAL.

A Moron Manager will go to any lengths to avoid anxiety and inadequacy, using a whole set of mental exercises that allows them to pretend they're really doing well, when basically they suck. Some of this denial comes in the form of the lies they live. Some of it comes through the abuses they heap onto others. Here's a personal example. In my work, I travel constantly, doing two or even three things at once all the time. Nevertheless, when I'm driving down the highway and talking to clients, I put the coffee down, pick up the hand-set, and discuss matters with them as if they were the most important person in the world. This is the way I recommend that my clients talk to others, too, demonstrating a core value (e.g., respect and interest). But if I'm honest with myself, I recognize that I treat my client respectfully not because I'm such a wonderful human being, but because I know I had better be a good boy in the role of service provider.

How do I know? Well, when I'm on the road talking to my assistant, I'm on the speaker phone, chomping on a bagel, and slurping an orange juice, yelling at other drivers and interrupting her to rant about airport delays. My assistant, God bless her, probably feels like she's talking to a heifer in advanced stages of Mad Cow Disease.

Innocuous enough? Think about what I'm really saying to her and imagine the mental gymnastics that I—someone who is supposed to be vigilant about this stuff for a living—have to engage in to allow myself to get away with it. Firstly, it reveals that I've made a fundamental decision that my assistant cannot hurt me, which by definition means that I have power over her; and secondly, I've decided that my position of power entitles me to be lazy and disrespectful. If asked whether or not I was a good manager, however, I'd probably say, "You bet!" and add that it's because of my ability to deal with people.

How can I fool myself so thoroughly? I can deny it like this: I'd say that my assistant knows me and knows I don't mean anything wrong by it; that the demands of the job require that I let go sometimes; I'm only human; I was in a tight squeeze on that particular day and had no time to eat except while I doubled that up with taking care of business with her. Still, I wouldn't do it to my client, so I know it's wrong on some level. My role as manager allows me to say that this transgression, under these circumstances, is not really representative of who I am. Well, if there were two excuses I could proclaim a Moron Manager should never ever be allowed to use, they would be:

"It wasn't really me"

And

"That's not who I 'really' am"

Until those excuses are banned, there's no reason why a Moron Manager will ever have to change who they really are.

Sudden Derailment
(When a moron manager's world turns upside down)

Shining stars. Every down-on-their-luck Moron Manager was one once a Golden Boy, a fast-tracker, a High-Potential "A-player." And every company needs to sustain what they're building through the people who will lead it in the next generation.

Think of an ascending executive, someone very young, who has been targeted for great things. Someone else in the organization has decided that this guy or gal has some potential. So a third person, usually a leadership development professional in HR that plans out a career track for the "Hi-Po" that includes regular and somewhat pre-planned promotions. Sure, it's all based on performance, but those promotions are anticipated nonetheless, an express lane to the top. Given all the odds, the ascending executive should be able to make it.

Except that somewhere along the line, the majority derails. They wind up either bumped out of the company or sidetracked into some staff job or demoted to some lower level position or shunted off to some dead-end subsidiary, because:

> *The things that made a Moron Manager great as a junior*
> *executive are the same things that kill them as they rise.*

That's right. A Moron Manager's sins come back to haunt them.

The denial, the self-aggrandizement, the selfishness, the general manner in which they treated other people on the way up, are the unwitting seeds of their very own destruction. But what's really remarkable is that the one-time golden child never sees that destruction coming. They are always surprised at their own derailment, and no one else ever is!

Why is it such a surprise to the poor Moron Manager? Because they've been told all along that they were doing the right thing. Their aggressiveness, toughness, cold-blooded decisiveness, and ruthlessness have been recognized, rewarded, and reinforced; but it's also been remembered. Everyone ends up hating them along the way. People wait in the wings for them to fail or do whatever they can to accelerate the fall. What's more, because the fast rising star doesn't recognize that he has got to change in midstream, that being a manager is different from being a leader, they walk right into the trap. The poor Moron Manager honestly didn't see it coming.

But you saw it, didn't you? Time and time again. Sure, the details varied depending on the individual, but the end result was always the same. Manager X—that hard-charging, results-producing, slave-driver—got ousted because his division's numbers mysteriously plummeted. Manager Y—the political insider who masterfully coordinated a corner office coup—ended up going nowhere because nobody trusted her enough to keep her in the loop anymore. Manager Z—the one that got put in charge of cutting the work force down by 30%—fell off the map after the merger... After all, who'd want to work with a ruthless person like that?

Investigate as many career wrecks as you'd like, you're going to come up with the same underlying cause. The number one predictor of derailment is interpersonal insensitivity: Being completely blind to how others see you, how you're affecting them, and what they really think about you. Moron Managers are simply not self-aware enough or courageous enough to look inward for the truth, or even, God forbid, seek out and take advantage of feedback from others. But they pay the price in the end.

It's not completely their fault. The organization developed them this way. But that doesn't mean it's not their responsibility to change—or their opportunity to grow—but the sad thing is that most Moron Managers think they're different. They honestly believe that they're not actually all that bad. They think their people understand what they really intend—deep in their hearts—no matter how they come across. Consequently they're pretty sure they'll get away with being a Moron Manager forever—and they almost never see what's coming to them until it's too late.

There is hope. Plenty of it. But before we even get to the point of helping a Moron Manager work on fixing their deep-seated interpersonal failings, we've got to get a lot more real first.

The Royal Road To Getting REAL
★ Waking Yourself Up ★

- ### Aim before you shoot!
  When you feel like questioning others, question yourself instead. Self-examination generates more possibilities with greater personal responsibility. So, instead of blaming others when things go wrong, take the blame yourself; and when things go right, give the credit away.

- ### Treat others like you really need them.
  Remember: You need your people more than they need you. Pretend that in ten years from now, your life will depend on someone you work with. Ask yourself, "How should I treat him today?" Give that a try and see how he responds. I bet you'll both like it... and get more done.

- ### Give your power away; you'll get it back with interest.
  Think of power as an expandable pie, not a limited resource. Enable others to surpass themselves by encouraging—if not demanding—autonomy and independence. When they ask for your help, coach them to find the best direction themselves!

Step 2

Getting REAL About You

Chapter Three

···

"Getting REAL"
or
Got a Problem? Get a Mirror!

So... we're almost to the top.

We've talked about your friend, the Moron Manager. We've talked about your BOSS, the Moron Manager. We've talked about me, the Moron Manager. We've talked about some Moron Managers in the news. And we've talked about some Moron Managers throughout history. But none of those people are reading this book. You are.

To get your money's worth, I think you'll agree, it's about time we started to talk about you.

If every book has a steep point that makes it hard to get over, this book's peak is coming up. Don't stop now. It will be worth it to get to the other side. I'm not saying that it will be all daisy fields and downhill treks once you get there, but you'll understand why it's so vital for you to continue the journey across the other peaks and valleys to come.

Are you ready?

Abracadabra!
(Or, how the magician reverse-engineered all those princes & princesses into hideous toads.)

For my next trick, I'm going to need a volunteer. Yes, I know that a lot of people out there— "your people," in fact—would dearly love to help me out with this, but right now it's just me and you. It's probably better that we're alone. Some tricks shouldn't be practiced in front of an audience.

Now we both know that magic is actually all just smoke and mirrors. But since we shouldn't be encouraging smoking, we'll just have to make do with the mirror.

Do you have one nearby? Any kind will do. You can use the really bright one in the bathroom that reveals your weary face in the morning or you can go to the full-length one in the hall that always flatters you when you're dressed up. If you're coming back to work from lunch and your office has reflective glass walls you can stand outside and see yourself there. Or, if you're a little worried about what comes next, you can sneak a peek into the hand held mirror you have in your desk drawer.

Hold this book up and take a long look into that mirror…

Ready?

Now, turn the page and read the following:

YOU ARE A MORON MANAGER, TOO.

Ouch! I know how much that hurts. I'm sorry that you feel betrayed. We were having so much fun laughing and complaining about all those real Moron Managers out there. So what's this accusation stuff all about, you're asking? Aren't we friends?

Yes. We are friends. In fact, I may be your best friend. You've never had anyone do you as good and kind and well meaning a favor as the one I'm doing for you now. You see, it was nearly too late. Remember all those Moron Managers we talked about who didn't see the career wreck that was coming their way? Well, guess what? That was your life right around the next curve. You probably don't believe me yet, but I'll provide the proof soon enough.

Still looking in the mirror? It's not that easy to do, is it? In fact, most people last only about 15 seconds gazing at themselves. While we've still got your attention, look a bit more closely. That's the face everyone who works for you sees every day…

Do you have any idea what they <u>really</u> think of you?

Buy Two Moron Manager Books (Get one moron free!)

A two for one special! If I had my way, that's the deal every bookstore would offer anyone buying this book.

You see, if you like this book a lot, I bet the first thing you'll want to do is give it to some "real" Moron Manager that you know. You might do it subtly by placing the book on the corner of your desk when they come in to see you. Or you might be sneaky and send it to them anonymously through the intra-company mail. Or you might be belligerent and scribble, "Read this, you Moron!" on a personal memo, stick it to the cover and hurl the book at them from across the room.

But will you be genuinely surprised when you get a copy back from someone else?

Try it, and tell me what happens…

See! No, it's not a boomerang; it's the truth! In fact, it's a message that people were trying to give you all along—one that you just chose to ignore. No matter how many people told you that you're a Moron Manager, you were immune to their complaints. It didn't matter if your employees under performed, pretended to like you, or left you as soon as they could for whatever job provided them with the slightest opportunity to flee. You thought that none of that applied to you as a person. The truth is, no matter what anyone says or does, you know you don't have to listen because you've got it all figured out in advance:

Whatever it is, it's all THEIR fault!

And my only reply to that is:

Got a problem?

Get a mirror!

Beginning To Question Yourself
(Instead of always questioning others)

You still don't believe me, yet. That understanding will take a while. But just for starters, when was the last time you seriously asked yourself, "Why did I treat this person that way?" Or, "What hot button of mine was just pushed that made me react like that?" Or, "Why am I forcing this decision on others? What is it that makes me comfortable and makes them resist?" If you're a Moron Manager, these and other vitally important, introspective questions never get asked, and the insight, the understanding, the self-awareness, not to mention the changes in attitude, behavior, and management style that might arise from the answers, never does.

We're so much quicker to question others than we are to question ourselves. Why? Because we naturally assume that we are right and others are wrong. The higher in rank a Moron Manager gets, the firmer that conviction becomes. No two people view reality the same way, however; both are equally right in their own minds. Try operating under that assumption for a change and see how different the world looks.

For example, remember that employee who under performed or left your group because he couldn't hack the pressure? Think about how you felt the last time you didn't meet a goal or left a situation for greener pastures. Unlike your employee:

- When you left your job for another company, it wasn't because of the money or the opportunity, the pressure or the demands of the job; it was because you had not been treated *as well as you deserved.*

• When you under performed, missed objectives, or otherwise failed to live up to expectations, it was not because of a lack of potential or ability, passion or focus; it was because you had not been treated *as well as you deserved.*

How did you deserve to be treated? Well, for starters, certainly not with the objective performance measures, personal disregard and general distance and toughness needed to handle subordinates. Instead, your performance would have been better if you had been treated with respect, consideration, compassion, empathy, supportiveness, and understanding.

Right?

Are you starting to get the picture? I hope so. Achieving that awareness is a giant first step towards becoming a genuinely decent human being who treats others as they deserve. You may not believe me yet, but no REAL Leader is anything less.

The Book of Pain & Self-Doubt (A REAL inspirational guide)

Let me repeat, this is not a process that is going to make you feel good—not at first. Nor is it a book that's going to pump you full of inspirational messages and send you back into the trenches eager to take on the world, not before you've paid your dues. The initial discomfort, anxiety, and awkwardness you are going to feel, however, is ultimately for the best. There's too much unwarranted, easily bought-and-sold, overly sunny and ultimately shallow optimism out there already. Check out any leadership book on the shelf of your local airport bookstore and you'll see what I mean. Just flipping through the pages will probably make you feel better right away. Too bad that's not going to make you a better leader.

But isn't self-esteem critical, you ask? Sure, self-confidence would be fine if we really earned and deserved it. But when we are unwilling to do the hard work necessary to see the mistakes we make and the problems we cause, we can only pretend to "get REAL" with others because we are not even being REAL with ourselves.

A Moron Manager knows how to play that role to the hilt. He buffers himself from self doubt by leaning on position, title, the corner-office, number of subordinates, size of budget, promotions, etc. Why do we rely on such excuses? We think that introspection takes too much time, self-doubt slows us down, and reflection paralyzes our ability to think and act clearly. But that's only because we are afraid of what real self-awareness would lead us to understand. We are unable to look in the mirror for too long because the difference between who we are and who we pretend to be is painful and frightening.

A REAL leader, on the other hand, is afraid of self-confidence because it breeds complacency and gets in the way of self-doubt. How's that for a paradox? Well, this book, as you're probably starting to notice, is full of them. Great leaders embrace self-doubt because it is the best tool available for being aware enough to change and grow as life and work demand. They know that title, position, and other external trappings mean nothing. They have learned that it is necessary to engage deliberately and actively in the internal process of "becoming the leader you're not" in order to have any REAL success.

What a Moron Manager Needs to Manage Most (Is the thing they manage least)

But before we get too excited, let's get back to being real. You're a good person—deep inside. So why do others see you as a Moron Manager? Was it the job that made you that way? Or should we look back and blame your upbringing, your parents, or your teachers?

All of the above. But that doesn't mean you didn't contribute to the whole mess. As a manager you don't even have the first clue what it is that you're actually managing.

Huh?

It's true. I make that bold claim right here, right now, without even knowing the slightest thing about you personally. I don't care what industry you're in, what position you hold, or how tough or soft you think you are. You may be the distribution manager or chief union buster in the most cut-throat, price-cutting, anti-competitive widget manufacturer in the world or the director of customer happiness and warm fuzzy feelings at the SQUEEZE-ME Stuffed Toy Company, it's still the same. You don't have a clue what it is you're managing and that's why you can't even *begin* to become a REAL leader.

Don't believe me? Take the Moron Manager Taste Test Challenge. If I ask you, "What is the single most important asset you have, the *numero uno* thing you need to manage?" I bet you will say the following:

MY PEOPLE

Don't feel too bad; 90% of Moron Managers say the same thing…

Because they think that they're enlightened.

And it's funny, isn't it, how far we've come with all this sentimental, touchy-feely, our-people-are-our-greatest-asset, New Age nonsense. We're steeped in it now. It's the air we breathe. We're so conditioned to think in knee-jerk fashion about "our people" that if our spouse woke us up in the middle of the night to check if we'd let the cat in, we'd probably sit up in bed still trapped in some corporate nightmare and yell, "My People! My People!" until he or she held us tenderly and we went back to sleep counting "human capital" sheep.

We _think_ we've made progress. We think we live and work at this very moment in an enlightened age of management (with the possible exception of how our own manager treats us). I suppose all managers have thought so since the dawn of time.

But, at least your heart is in the right place, even if your head is somewhere else. The genuinely scary Moron Managers talk like managers used to talk. When asked the same question that I asked you, about 5% of them will talk about their budget, resources, customer intimacy, or some other nonsense. Then there's another 5% or so who will come up with something a little more creative (just to show that they're hard and not soft), like their time or the financial well-being of the company or market position and shareholder value.

But I say to them, as I say to you now:

How does it feel to be completely wrong?

Because the single most important asset for you to manage is:

YOU

Simply put, there is only one asset you have complete 100% control over in your life and that asset is *you*. And if you don't manage *you*, how can you expect to manage anyone else? This is not a call to look in the mirror and admire your good looks. I'm not talking about the self-serving way you've been managing yourself without realizing it. I'm talking about managing the way you impact the people around you. This is a call to develop a clear understanding of how "what you do" to others hurts them and you, stifles your humanity, removes their interest in you, and undercuts your ability to lead.

When most managers are asked about what it is they need to manage most carefully, they list the external things. People. Customers. Resources. Finances. It's not surprising. As managers, the focus of our attention is typically outside of ourselves, at the things we supposedly need to impact or control to do our jobs. What we need as leaders, however, is to focus on our internal resources. It's the spring board towards honesty and a greater awareness of how we affect the people around us.

But it's far easier to look outside for excuses instead of inside for answers. Psychologists refer to this in Attribution Theory (the study of where we attribute the causes of things) as the "Fundamental Attribution Bias," a highly technical term for the basic human instinct to self-protect by diverting all blame and sources of failure elsewhere, while saving the credit for anything good that happens for our very own. It's what we all do to further our careers and it's a first class, grade-A recipe for management disaster.

When a subordinate is under-performing a Moron Manager blames that subordinate's inner stuffing. They say the person is lazy. Or that they lack what it takes. Or they are soft and do not have the killer instinct. Basically that they are, in some overly simplistic fashion, not emotionally cut-out for the job. But like everyone else, when a manager is called to task for one of his own failings, that manager is quick to provide a detailed explanation of the external excuses that made that failing, action, or attitude the appropriate one. They'll say, it's the way the organization is set up, i.e., the structure made me do it; or the reward system reinforces that, i.e., how can I be anything different when that's what they pay me for?

But it's not the structure or the reward system that makes a Moron Manager act as they do. Not ultimately. Faceless organizations can't be blamed for everything. Individuals are the ultimate initiator of their actions. A human hand flicks the switch, signs the release form or fails to give a pat on the back. It's the rare occasion when someone actually forces you to do the things you do. It's all too often the case that you do those things willingly, even eagerly, out of your own urge for self-preservation and self-promotion.

Leaders don't blame outside forces, external factors, or overarching conspiracies for their actions. Leaders know deep inside that *they* are ultimately responsible for the bad things that happen around them as much as the good. In fact, if leaders have an attribution bias it leans towards the other extreme: They feel that they are an instrumental factor in everything which occurs around them, even when those things are removed from their direct impact. It's an accountability obsession, a tendency to feel others' pain, failure, remoteness or distraction as due to some cause created by themselves, combined with an eagerness to give the credit for success, achievement, or high performance to the person who did the deed and most deserves the acclaim.

If you want to turn your own self-serving behavior around, the place to start is within. You need to become aware of yourself, of your own self-centered biases and motives, in order to become conscious of how you affect the world around you. All Moron Managers are guilty of this. All leaders have learned to become who they're not by dealing first with the truth of who they are.

Don't get me wrong. It's not as if focusing on the external world is a bad thing. It's just not the place to begin. Leaders start from inside. It's why they are able to take full responsibility for themselves. Managers focus on the outside from the get-go, avoiding the inner work by concentrating on their people, their resources, their financial numbers. As a result, they end up being fundamentally unable to accept any responsibility at all.

When the cookie jar falls from the counter and breaks, the first thing a child will do is pretend it never happened. Confronted with the reality of the broken jar, the child will blame anyone or anything for the reason it fell, no matter how absurd or irrational the explanation. It was the little brother, the cat, the wind, the cupboard door… or, my own personal favorite, it fell all by itself. Think about how hard it is, even now as an adult, to act like one and say, "Yes, it was me. I broke the cookie jar. I made a mistake and have no excuse, no way to lessen the blame by diverting it elsewhere."

Leaders accept the blame and take the hit because they've grown into the types of people who understand the consequences of their own actions. Moron Managers, like all children, want those cookies more than life itself. If the cookie jar should happen to fall in the process, you can be certain that they will point the finger elsewhere to avoid the responsibility.

Overcoming the Moron Manager Within
(To become the leader you're not)

You're not yet a leader because you never learned how to become one. No one taught you that it was important to develop those skills. Your organization is not even telling you now that it will reward you for doing so no matter how beneficial it would be to everyone you work with. But your life is the poorer for it and your world is, too. It's time to make a break from that and become the leader you're not.

During this temporary phase of weakness, I want to acknowledge the pain and anxiety involved in such change and let you know up front that I recognize that it's not your fault. None of it. You didn't create the family you grew up in or the organization that developed you. But that doesn't mean that it's not your responsibility or your opportunity for growing past it. DO NOT FEEL GUILTY. You're not the cause of this outcome, but act as though you are, and take advantage of the opportunity you have now.

Remember this, and say it to yourself whenever you need to:

It's not my fault,
but it is my problem.

This is your opportunity to get better and I urge you to embrace it. That's what a leader does—all the time. At some level, they are eternally dissatisfied. For them, good enough never is. They are always in self-improvement mode, not as a process or exercise but as a way of life. For Moron Managers, self-improvement is a technique to get ahead, a course to take, a book to read or a set of new ideas to use. That's an important difference, a distinction between an internalized activity and an externalized one, a genuine search versus a tool.

A real leader understands that leadership is not natural. For them, getting REAL means not allowing for convenient and cowardly escape clauses. Part of the way a leader does this is by asking for the help of those around them. It's a simple but profound shift in the way we relate to others. Once the people around us know who we are and what values we stand for, they become our partners and helpers, supporting and encouraging our adherence to those values rather than using them as a way to entrap us.

None of this comes easily. In order to initiate the process of "Becoming the Leader You're Not," you've got to begin by admitting

"I'm Not Satisfied With Who I Am." That doesn't mean that you dislike everything about you or that you're a fundamentally rotten person, but it does mean that there are parts of you which need to change. It's time to understand why they are a source of pain to you and others.

Being so open and self-aware will feel strange at first, as awkward as it did the first time you rode a bicycle. That's okay, too. It's what growth and change are all about even if, as adults, we don't remember what that feels like. The goal, however, is profoundly worthwhile. You will come to understand the powerful role of true self-awareness, the value of living with a constant shadow, a part of yourself that functions as your own mentor and critic, a source of strength rather than something to be avoided.

But all that comes later. We've still got to get REAL about who you are first. It's not until the third section of the book that you will learn how you can build from a new place to become the leader—or rather the *person*—you're not.

It's never too late. But it does have to be done in earnest. You only come through here once. You should at least play as if the score counts.

The Royal Road To Getting REAL
★ Self-Reflection: The Only Way To Start Looking Better ★

- **Self-doubt is the foundation of REAL leadership.**
  Get REAL with others by first getting REAL with yourself. Acknowledge and own your strengths, but also acknowledge and own your limitations. Pack your world with people who shoulder your liabilities and can benefit from your strengths.

- **The most important thing you need to manage is you.**
  And the part that's most critical is your true emotional impact on others. Not what you think you produce, not what you want to produce, but the consequences you create.

- **Your people are your partners... not your tools for implementation.**
  Tools can repair cars and tools can build houses, but only your people can help you to understand, adhere to, and live your leadership values. As partners, you have the potential to bring out the best in each other. Use this partnership as a "leadership mirror"— to be a REAL leader.

Chapter Four

....

Truth & Consequences
or
"Your People" Are Not As Dumb As You'd Like Them to Be

Time for another fairy tale. Do you remember the children's story, *The Emperor's New Clothes*? This story goes kind of like that one.

Once upon a time, there was this manager who ran a kingdom somewhere and wanted some really good looking clothes to make himself look particularly "managerial."

So he ordered a tailor to make them. His demands were so unrealistic, however, that the tailor only pretended to work. Instead of making new clothes, the tailor relied on the manager's obvious vanity to convince him he looked great in his new uniform, even though that uniform was only pretend and the manager wasn't wearing anything at all. Could the manager really be so blind? Well, he thought he must look pretty good, if the tailor said he did.

Bursting with pride and ego, the manager gathered all his people together to show off his new look. His people, unwilling to point out his condition, held back the truth and applauded as if the manager were the greatest, best-dressed leader in the world.

Except for one little boy, who didn't know any better. That little boy pointed and said:

"What the heck are all of you talking about? This manager's not wearing a uniform! He's buck naked!"

At which point, everyone else started laughing and pointing, too. The manager looked down and saw that it was true. He went back to his office in shame and embarrassment, never to reveal himself again. The tailor, realizing that the gig was up, slinked out of town, and opened a small boutique managerial consulting firm which thrives to this very day.

I only wish it were a fairy tale. But it's not. That's the awful, embarrassing, and painful truth I have to relay next. You've heard what I had to say thus far, and as a result you've developed a clearer picture of the weaknesses in your managerial style. You've wiped the sweat from your brow and said, "Boy, this 'Becoming the Leader I'm

Not' stuff is really tough. *Good thing I found out about my failings, incompetence, and self-delusion before everyone else did!*"

Well, I'm sorry to be the first to tell you but somebody had to…

You're standing buck naked before the world.

Feel the breeze?

You thought you were getting away with being a Moron Manager—but you're not. Everyone else has known all about it for a long, long time. Your most private acts have been on public display. The good news is, since pain is a precursor to enlightenment, you can at least be satisfied that you're going to feel *reeeeaallllly* enlightened soon.

Something had to inspire you to change. Maybe finally understanding that the things you do are observed by everyone else around you will help. After all, public embarrassment has its uses. In medieval times, they used to shame people for being lousy citizens by locking them up in the stocks in the middle of the town square. Who knows? Maybe they were on to something.

Because telling you how great you look certainly won't help get you over the hump. After all, it hasn't so far. The development plans, the courses, the leadership books, the 360° feedback sessions—none of those things have impacted you in the slightest, have they? The interpersonal skill development you need is not going to come without a major shock to your system. Real internal change needs a tad more work than you'll feel compelled to do through supportive ego stroking. You're not going to alter your entire personality by attending some nice weekend Executive-Team-Building/Outward-Bound-style retreat. Just because you tug on ropes, eat beans from a can, scrape your knee, sunburn half your face, and fall into some trusted colleague's loving arms, doesn't mean you won't stab that very same colleague in the back as soon as you return to the office.

No, just knowing that everyone, everyday, sees you naked in all your glory, ought to help. At least, you won't be able to fool yourself that you're getting away with it anymore.

Your People Know Who You Are (They are not as dumb as you'd like them to be.)

Your people are better at seeing you than you are at seeing yourself.

Don't believe me? Try this test. Choose a Moron Manager colleague in your organization, find that manager's subordinates, get them together in a room, play some soft music to make them feel relaxed, dim the lights to enhance concentration, and ask them the following penetrating questions about their wonderful leader:

- What time does your manager get to work in the morning?
- What kind of shirts does your manager wear on which days?
- How does your manager take his coffee?
- What time of day is your manager in his worst mood?

Trivial? You'll probably think so before asking. But when you hear their answers-immediate, detailed, and chillingly consistent- the truth will begin to dawn on you.

They're watching...

Now for Part Two of the test. Go to that Moron Manager and ask him those very same questions. What time do those pesky subordinates arrive in the morning? How do they take their coffee? What clothes do they wear for the big presentation?

Is the poor Moron Manager at a loss? Well, let's not be too tough. Tell them they don't need to know all the answers, just some. It's not a race, they can take their time, and any answer will do...

Still waiting?

They don't have a clue, do they? And neither do you about your own people.

That's why you thought you were safe.

Feel the breeze?

Moron Managers go through most of their careers as if what they do does not have any effect on those around them. They behave as if they are invisible or operating in some kind of interpersonal vacuum. They don't realize that they are constantly under surveillance by the people who look to them for leadership.

If you have one illusion dispelled by this book, let it be this one: Managers are never invisible. When it comes to "their people," they are always under the microscope.

Understand what I'm saying? You are being watched. Closely.

It's an alarming thought, isn't it? In fact, it's so frightening, I bet you have two panicky, self-serving bursts of concern running through your brain simultaneously right now.

- "What did they see? What shameful acts have I committed, supposedly in the dark, that were actually done in full view of everyone around me?"

And

- "Why? Why are they watching me so closely? What have I ever done to deserve that?"

I'll answer the second concern first.

You're their leader. Not in any REAL sense, but as sad as it is, you're all they've got, and they look to you for answers. They're watching you as closely as they can for consistency of message, some clue as to what you stand for and what matters most to you, some signal as to how they should behave in order to please you, anticipate your direction, live up to your expectations, rules, guidelines and boundaries.

Surprised? I bet. Who knew they took you so seriously?

Now that you've been exposed to that little shocker, let's move on to another one. Since (a) you didn't know they were watching, and (b) you didn't know that they were looking to you for meaningful guidance, what kind of guidance/message/signal have you been inadvertently conveying all this time about what it is you stand for and how you want them to behave?

I'm afraid you can answer that one yourself. Simply refer back to your first concern and think about all the shameful acts you've been committing, supposedly in the dark, all the time.

Breezy, isn't it!

The Moron Manager's First Principle of Power (Do unto others whatever you can get away with.)

Interpersonal Insensitivity is at the core of a Moron Manager's problem. That means you are blind to:

- How others see you
- How what you do dramatically affects them
- What "your people" really think of you
- How all of that impacts the commitment, communication, and contribution they offer you in return

Here's how it happened and why you permitted yourself to

become that way.

As you made your way up the ranks and became more "senior," you also became—via your words, attitudes and acts—more and more interpersonally insensitive, less and less aware of how others see you, increasingly indifferent as to how you affect them, and gradually disinterested in treating them as fellow human beings.

Why? Because as you accumulated position, prestige, control, and territory, you also accumulated the power to hurt those around you- a power that "your people" in turn don't have over you, except maybe in passive aggressive forms.

Surprised at the bluntness of that? You shouldn't be. After all, that's the basic truth at the heart of the manager-subordinate relationship. The manager has the power to hurt the subordinate, and the subordinate needs to be obsequious, pleasant, and eager to please because establishing a veneer of trust, compassion, and mutual reliance in the relationship is the only chance he has of not getting stomped.

And you thought they just liked you! That you could do no wrong because you were such a people person! That your ideas and comments and plans and observations were brilliant because everyone told you so!

There's that breeze again.

The relationship between boss and subordinate starts to change when that power dynamic shifts. Look at volunteer groups for example. When you can't fire the people around you, withhold their paychecks, derail their career paths, give them lousy evaluations, or shunt them aside to dead-end roles, when you need them more than they need you, you find yourself treating them a whole lot better. Suddenly, they're not *human capital*, they're *human beings*.

Leaders treat their people as if they are volunteers—all the time. That's a significant component of the different way they approach work relationships. They know that, ultimately, people do have choices; in fact, they can choose how much of their passion, loyalty, commitment, creativity, focus, effort, and heart they want to apply to their work.

Treating your employees as if they are volunteers became something of a mantra in recent years—but it's not going to stick, and it didn't really mean anything in the first place. When the "War for Talent" (nice term, don't you think, for drawing people towards you?) was at its height, profit sharing, work-life balance, extracurricular activities, meaningful volunteer opportunities, casual work environments, flattened hierarchies, telecommuting, flexible hours, daycare, laundry facilities, Friday afternoon beer gardens, sales trips to Aruba, in-house massages, spontaneous floor hockey games, giant hot tubs, professional rock climbing walls, group yoga, and all kinds of other misplaced substitutes for just treating people decently, became all the rage. But that will all be out the door when the economy changes, which it always does. It's already started. Witness the last deep cuts in work force (and note how few CEOs have yet to be laid off for their accountability), the return to the "discipline" of formal Fridays, the cutting of benefits, bonuses, and perks for everyone but the senior team whose salaries keep rising! All those "Come Work For Us Because We're So Employee Friendly" messages are silent now that the power relationship between employer and employee has altered dramatically again. The world that had been upside down, is righting itself once more.

And why should we be surprised? It's not as if all those Moron Managers saw the light or truly understood what they'd been doing wrong. There was no deep gut check on human values, no internalization of the lessons of what it really takes to attract and keep the best. The changes made were never very meaningful anyway. Take a look at what David Owens of Vanderbilt University found when he examined 35,000 e-mail exchanges at a hip, new economy organization in which there were self-formed, self-managed, voluntary work teams, no titles and no ostensible hierarchy.

Despite the flatness of the organization, it wasn't difficult to pick out who was in charge. Workers at the bottom end of the scale used e-mail predominantly as a means of building relationships. They forwarded jokes, gave compliments, made social plans, flirted.

Mid-level employees wrote the longest and most detailed work-related e-mails. To even the simplest concerns, they gave extensive arguments that were well-formulated but wordy and occasionally argumentative, cc'ing everyone involved, spell checking before hitting the dreaded "Send All" button. It was part of their ongoing, daily need to make political points, build group consensus, foster allies, influence opinions, those things we need to do when we can't just snap our fingers and make people jump, but need to convince, cajole, fool, enthuse, and encourage instead.

And senior managers, those very people who praised themselves so glowingly for their "electronic accessibility" and democratic team-oriented work style, took the longest time to answer, paid the least attention to the content of the message they were replying to, used uneven capitalization and poor spelling and grammar, "conveying the sense that they had better things to do with their time."

("How To E-Mail Like a CEO," by Bruce Headlam, New York Times, Sunday Times Magazine, April 9, 2001.)

Intentions
(And actions)

I'm sure those senior executives didn't mean to come across as disdainful or indifferent, that's just how it got interpreted by those around them. Deep inside they know how they really meant to come across, that's what provides them with all the excuses they'll ever need to behave that way again in the future.

And therein lies the problem. You see, as human beings we're all guilty of this one:

We judge others by their actions,
but we judge ourselves by our intentions

For example, consider this scenario. You're walking down the street and you notice a tall man with blond hair, glasses, and a black briefcase standing outside a fashionable clothing store display window, licking the glass.

Your first reaction is that this guy is nuts. Then, because you're so smart, you give it more thought and come to the conclusion that the man is a sexual deviant whose lid or cover has blown and whose fetish for mannequins wearing women's evening gowns has finally gotten the better of him on an otherwise leisurely early afternoon commute home from work.

A not unreasonable assumption, given the available facts.

But if you stop and ask that man why he's licking the window he might say something like, "Well, you see that TV camera over there across the street? They're paying me a thousand dollars to be bold enough to do it."

This makes his actions seem a little more reasonable than you first thought. Heck, if the market had a particularly bad day, you might be tempted to start French kissing the window yourself.

The point of the story is this:

We look "outside" ourselves (external) for an
explanation of our own behavior...
but we look inside (internal) for an explanation
of other people's behavior.

Which means that while the licking window man saw his actions as perfectly rational given the external reinforcement, you, as the admittedly shocked bystander, were unable to see any possibility beyond the certainty that he was nuts. You saw his motivations as internally focused around his own strange urges, rather than externally centered on a quick cash payoff.

Now think about the messages you've sent over the years. What seemingly minor crimes, which made complete sense to you, have you committed without realizing it?

What about all those occasions you said, "Get your work in on time," instead of, "Turn in something that matters." Or those times when you berated someone for not working on Saturdays instead of praising them for the creative solutions they came up with on a day off. Or whenever you chastised someone for taking a full hour for lunch instead of suggesting that they take someone else in the group out in order to foster a better relationship. You may think all of that is unimportant. You may actually believe that the underlying intention of your action—your desire that your people perform at top levels— was understood loud and clear, but it wasn't. Not even close. If you don't believe me, ask them. Or think about it this way: If someone else treated *you* the same way *you* treat *your* subordinates, how would you feel? I bet you'd resent it. As a shrewd "up-and-comer," you might not be open about that resentment, but you'd *know* that they'd done it and you wouldn't forget—and it isn't too likely you'd put your best efforts forward to help this person in the future—not in any meaningful, heartfelt way. Instead you'd probably embrace the biggest moron management credo of them all:

It isn't enough for me to succeed…
it's important that others fail, too.

Is there a disconnect in all this? A little hypocrisy between your position as victim and your role as victimizer? You bet. But that's only because you don't have a clue what it really means to care about "your people" in the first place. How do I know? Well, if you really cared, you wouldn't be so worried about yourself right now; you'd be *horrified* at what you did to them.

So, in the future, because you are not naturally inclined to figure out how other people feel about the things you do to them, or why what they do bothers you, you should tattoo the following two questions to some handy part of your anatomy so as to not commit your crimes again:

Do my intentions match my actions?
Do my actions match the consequences?

That's Not Who I Really Am
(And other Moron Manager excuses)

Does any of this sound like you? Do you have any gaps between your intentions and your actions? Are you guilty of interpersonal insensitivity?

You might not be willing to admit it, yet, but I bet you've got your excuses all lined up just in case. To get it over with, please choose from one of the three following options and receive your instant rebuttal.

EXCUSE #1:
"I'm only human."

Being human is a funny excuse for being disdainful and indifferent. In fact, I just wish you were human enough to see what you do to other human beings. If you want an excuse that really works here, simply admit that you are weak, lazy, and self-indulgent. We can work on that, and you'll have been honest for a change, too.

EXCUSE #2:

"I may be that way at work but I'm not like that at home."

Which gives us, at the very least, the opportunity to hospitalize you, since there's a technical term for such a condition and it's known as "Split Personality."

But you don't really need the strait jacket because you don't actually change personalities when you take the suit jacket off at home. That's just another form of self-deception on your part. Don't believe me? Well, let's ask your spouse and children a few questions about how you act around the house. Sure, that's not how you intended what you do to be interpreted, but that's how it came across.

Still, the fact that you think being a manager is a role, is part of the problem. Leaders don't operate as if their job is a role-they work in their job as if they are living their life.

EXCUSE #3:

"I'm not the only Moron Manager out there."

It's true. They taught you everything they know. And it's also true that there are other people out there who are probably even worse than you, as if that should make it all better. After all, what a great inspirational recruiting slogan that would be: "Join us! We're no worse than the other guys!"

But you're guiltier than most because you are in a position of power and "leadership." You agreed to this role, desired it, went after it, and accepted it. Yet, your actions have had a significant, negative impact on the people around you, particularly those who look to you for support, guidance, recognition, direction, and vision.

You've never given any of that a second thought, however. Even now, as the list of characteristics accumulate, I bet you are still thinking more of the people you know who are Moron Managers than the manager you are and the hurtful things that you have done.

If so, you're not alone.
But you will be someday.

Just for kicks, let's take a look at some other real life Moron Managers and see if they ring any bells.

Fasten your seatbelt. Keep your mirror handy. We're going to make a visit to the Moron Managers' Hall of Shame.

The Royal Road To Getting REAL
* Under the Microscope *

- **Your people are more observant of you than you could ever be of them.**

   Never underestimate how many people are constantly monitoring your activities. They're looking for some consistency or pattern which communicates who you are and what you stand for. They will exploit any inconsistencies you reveal. Be damned careful!

- **Leaders treat their people as if they are volunteers—because that's what they really are.**

   If the last economic downturn (2001-2003) showed us anything, it's how Moron Managers systematically abuse people who they feel are held hostage. If you ever say to yourself, "They can't go anywhere else," then you should.

- **The only way to measure your intentions is by examining the effects of your actions.**

   Abandon your proclivity to excuse egregious behavior as being well-intended. Intentions may be the balm of salvation for Moron Managers, but not for REAL leaders. Lead like what you actually do matters.

....

Chapter Five

The Moron Managers' Hall of Shame
or
Your Future Home Should You Choose to Reside There

To Be
(Or not to be)

Rest assured, no one is forcing you to become the leader you're not. Even now, having read this book to this point, you don't have to take one shred of the self-knowledge made available to you and do anything about it. I can't even guarantee that anything bad will happen to you tomorrow as a result. I can, however, promise that if you don't follow the prescribed steps in the last section of this book, someone out there will submit the evidence of your life long career for our consideration and nominate you to the:

Moron Managers' Hall of Shame

Step right in. Don't be shy. All of the crazed monsters and hideous creatures you see standing before you are actually skillfully crafted likenesses. They won't bite… not in here… they will not be able to hurt you… but that doesn't mean they're not scary.

Actually, what you might find most scary is how often you come across people like this in your own everyday working life. Some of them are your bosses, your peers and colleagues, your friends, and still others will just remind you of yourself. Well, we'll save that one for later.

Prepare for some strong reactions. You might hate some of these people and think they should be strung up for their crimes. Or you might like some of these people, especially the ones most resemble yourself, and feel that no matter how awful they look in the cold, harsh light, their intentions were good, and their hearts were in the right places.

Big Daniel

Daniel is six foot four, two hundred and twenty pounds and speaks in a charming southern drawl. His easy going style won't fool you for long, however, because Daniel has a fierce intensity about him that shows he "means" business.

He used to yell and scream a lot, use four letter words and throw things, but he discovered "religion" to some degree a few years back and doesn't do that anymore. He's proud of how much he's grown, and is the first (and only) one to inform you of his new enlightened self and 21st Century Management Style. But, he gets a little twinkle in his eye when he waxes nostalgic about how bad he used to be, back in the good old days, when "no-nonsense" was common sense, and mauling your employees was the sport of the day.

Daniel's favorite new age word is *accountability*. It's become his stock in trade, his personal mantra. As manager of his group, he believes in holding people accountable... because a great leader doesn't allow for excuses.

It's obvious that, despite his apparently civilized demeanor, Daniel's team is totally intimidated by him. Even Daniel recognizes it, but believes it to be their fault. Still, he tries hard to get people to participate on an equal footing.

For example, during group evaluations of all the members of his team (including himself), he told his people not to be afraid of the truth, that the pain of finding out what others really think of them is worth it because it will teach them a powerful, first-hand lesson about *accountability*.

Daniel is so enlightened. As person after person went through the process of leaving the room while the rest of the team evaluated them, Daniel gleefully led the way in providing honest, helpful feedback with "tough but fair" ratings. He was really good at it and could package the truth in a way that was helpful to the person receiving the news. He loved it… until his own turn came.

After Daniel's results came in and the news was shared with him, the veins started popping out on his temples. His eyes turned red. He pounded his fist on the table and proclaimed that the entire process was the most unfair thing poor Daniel had ever seen.

His scores were not terrible. They were not 1s or 2s, but they weren't 9s or 10s, either. In fact, they were fair-to-middling, indicating that although he was skilled in some areas, his people thought he needed a lot of work in others.

He insisted that he was going to resign. If his goddamn people thought he really deserved an average score of 6.4, then he had no business leading them.

It was difficult watching such a complete narcissist decompose publicly, attacking everyone and everything he could blame; but that was *nothing* compared to what came next, literally. Daniel took *nothing* from the lesson that he was given, heard *nothing* from the messages he was sent, and learned *nothing* from the pain he felt. To this day Daniel claims that the process, while fair for everyone else who went through it, was horribly slanted and deliberately skewed when it came to him. That's how fully Daniel has managed to suppress the truth, inflate his abilities, ignore the consequences, and deny the reality of his own leadership style, and its impact on others.

Here was an opportunity for Daniel to swallow his pride, look at his group and say, "I know you want some things from me that I'm not providing; you've made that clear. In the spirit of being *accountable,* I'm going to hold myself to that same standard and change."

However, he couldn't do it. He still has not been able to absorb that information and take such a forward step, even now, several years later. Because *accountability* is not a two-way street for Moron Managers—it's a modern weapon. If not paired with caring and support, *accountability* is nothing but a punitive concept, a hammer hanging overhead that let's people know they are not going to get away with anything without getting bludgeoned. After all, *accountability* is something that occurs after the fact, and what good is that? If a truck brimming with diesel fuel is coming up fast behind you on the highway, would you rather that driver were *accountable* or responsible? *Accountable* is not going to feel very meaningful to you when they're cleaning up after the accident.

That's how your employees feel. What's so sad is that when Daniel reads the story above, he'll think I've written about someone else! Poor, Daniel.

Sweet Jane

Jane's a star. She's risen to the top at a number of large corporations during her career and is currently a senior executive of Human Resources.

She's smart and interpersonally skilled. She conducts herself well, but she holds her jobs for only about 2 or 3 years on average before leaving in an emotional, bridge-burning huff. Why? She always ends up in companies ruled by autocratic men whom she can never ever please (not unlike her family dynamic). It's amazing how bad her luck is, continually running into these tyrants and creeps in some kind of perpetual nightmare from which she can't awaken. Too bad, it's all her own fault. Strike that... it's not her fault... but it is her problem.

Jane's been here more than once. In fact, she's always been in the same place. She just keeps changing partners. It started with her father, a man for whom she could never be good enough. To this day, she selects the same kinds of bosses to work for, men who are borderline psychopaths, hostile, dictatorial, arbitrary, and cruel. Just like Dad!

It goes well enough at the beginning. She knows how to handle these men to a point. She's willing and able to put up with their abuse and rises through the ranks accordingly. Yet, she knows the trouble is beginning all over again when she gets so resentful that she starts bad mouthing the boss.

One boss ago, it got to the point where every time she met with him, she would bring a pad of paper with her, write down everything that was said, and make him sign the notes as a way of confirming that the recorded details were what he had said and promised. With her current boss, she still manages to maintain a civil tone on the surface, but she found herself, as she got off the phone with him, muttering "Fuck you," just before the receiver hit the cradle. She didn't realize that all this hostility turned in on herself. It's the reason she ended up feeling as if she was not good enough and could never please her Moron Managers. Instead of acknowledging that truth, she quit, moved to a new company, and began the cycle all over again.

Now, Jane is smart and psychologically, a pretty healthy woman. She even grasps what she's doing to an extent and recognizes the pattern. But why does she keep it up, and how does she, time after time, wind up working for men who are not normal, in companies that are sick?

None of Jane's stupidity is going to get better until she makes a deliberate effort to change. It's not even as simple as finding a healthy company with a normal boss… she's probably not ready for that. She first needs to let go of something incredibly precious and dear to her—namely, her need for approval from someone that is going to withhold it.

That won't happen until Jane gets some things straight. The need for approval is fine, but unless Jane is able to pair that with someone who is going to provide that approval in a supportive manner, she's never going to get better. The problems that are holding her back and causing her and those around her pain are never going to go away. Ever.

Slippery Simon

Simon is European, proving that our continental cousins are not any more sophisticated at this management game than the rest of us. Simon is very savvy and very polished, but he's despised by his peers and his "underlings," as he calls them, because he is pompous, self-protective, and viciously accusatory whenever anything goes wrong. Unfortunately, he's very smart. That fact, coupled with his interpersonal vitriol, is a surefire guarantee of doom! The irony is, because Simon hires people who are sycophants, those abhorrent yes-men and women, he thinks that everyone loves him... when they are really just kissing the stitching on his shiny Italian silk suit.

If you ever have a chance to talk with Simon, you'll quickly find out how wonderful he is. Besides setting records for using the word "I" in consecutive sentences, he has built a great team, hired wonderful people, turned his company's fortunes around and single-handedly saved the European Market... all because of his broad intellectual abilities, his sophisticated interpersonal skills and his strategic mindset.

It was therefore a major surprise to Simon when he got axed. Please note that although it was a surprise, it was not a shock—certainly not in the something-must-be-wrong-with-me-so-I-must-examine-myself-closely-and-determine-what-that-is way. Anyone around Simon could have predicted his derailment (many did) because he is a manipulative slime. To this day, despite direct messages to the contrary, Simon thinks that it was a political move, designed to knock him down because his terrific success and wonderful capabilities were threatening those above him.

In fact, Simon's so blind to the truth that he has asked for references from people who openly despise him. I hear he's still looking for work.

Paul the Player

Paul is a senior VP of sales. He's a great guy, a very personable, slap 'em on the back and look after 'em kind of manager. He really loves people, he'll be quick to tell you, and the truth is… he really does. He has a pretty good heart.

What Paul hates is "all that political shit." What he means by "political" is the *tendency for others* (of course) to say what's appropriate instead of what's REAL; pick up on the appropriate way to behave by paying close attention to what people are doing; and weasel into power in a manner that doesn't reveal that power is the goal.

All of those deceitful, insincere, and underhanded behaviors drive him crazy. His virulence over this is curious, to say the least, because when you talk to Paul, a few things quickly become crystal clear… No one reads social situations more minutely. No one looks more closely for nuance of expression, gesture, and message. And, no one hedges more carefully what they really think, feel, or believe.

You might find it surprising that Paul is good at what he hates the most—it is, however a typical experience (I'll explain why later). For now, you should know that this blindness in Paul to his own interpersonal weakness is killing him, figuratively, in the sense that it's negatively affecting his career, and maybe even literally, as it relates to his physical health.

His political behavior is not overt or malicious, but it is protective and self-defeating. At the very least, it's causing him a lot of inner conflict, draining extremely important emotional energy, and causing him physical bad health, and high levels of anxiety. It holds him back from doing things that he knows he should. For example, when you ask Paul why he doesn't do something about the "political shit" going on in his company, he answers, "Because it wouldn't be appropriate." He has no clue that he's feathering his own nest, saving his own tail, politicking with the best of them in extremely sophisticated ways...

Everyone else sees it as clear as day. They know that Paul is a Player. They know that he can't be trusted.

Neal L. Patterson, CEO, Cerner Corporation

Up until now, we've been using pseudonyms to protect the guilty... but here comes someone you might actually know.

Poor Neal Patterson. Talk about public shaming. His abusive, disdainful, unreasonable, misdirected moronitude has been inadvertently revealed in all its glory, not just to the entire staff of his successful health care software development company, but to Wall Street analysts and shareholders, and anyone who read the front page of the business section of the New York Times on April 5, 2001.

You see, Neal got into work the morning of March 13, 2001, early, as he always does, and felt miffed that the Kansas City-based staff wasn't working hard enough. How did he know? The parking lot, at 7:45 AM, was hardly full. Sensing, as "leaders" do, that something needed to be done to turn things around and whip people into shape, Neal wrote a motivational e-mail to the company's 400 company managers in order to fix matters. It read:

> We are getting less than 40 hours of work from a large number of our K.C.-based EMPLOYEES. The parking lot is sparsely used at 8 a.m.; likewise at 5 p.m. As managers—you either do not know what your EMPLOYEES are doing; or you do not care. You have created expectations on the work effort which allowed this to happen inside Cerner, creating a very unhealthy environment. In either case, you have a problem and you

will fix it or I will replace you.

Never in my career have I allowed a team which worked for me to think they had a 40-hour job. I have allowed YOU to create a culture which is permitting this. NO LONGER.

And, according to the article, Neal's message continued to get worse. The *Times* author writes:

> *Mr. Patterson went on to list six potential punishments including laying off 5 percent of the staff in Kansas City. "Hell will freeze over," he vowed, before he would dole out more employee benefits. The parking lot would be his yardstick of success, he said; it should be "substantially full" at 7:30 a.m. and 6:30 p.m. on weekdays and half full on Saturdays.*
>
> *"You have two weeks," he said. "Tick, tock."*

The article didn't say whether the company parking lot was any fuller now, but it did mention that the company's stock price dropped 22 percent three days after Neal's e-mail was posted on one of Yahoo's public electronic message boards.

Could it be that shareholders sensed that Neal wasn't much of a leader... or that he wasn't, at the very least, going to have many followers in the near future? Hmmm. What do you think?

Certainly, as a classic Moron Manager, Neal is highly skilled and has most of the best tricks down cold. He noticed something he didn't like and acted decisively. Clearly, if the parking lot was not full mornings, nights, and weekends, this could mean only one thing—*people were slacking.* The fact that the lot was not full had to be the fault of *every manager in the company other than himself.* As such, he applied helpful guidance for improving the situation *telling managers that they must do "something" to fix the problem that they had created.*

Then he set up a series of rewards and punishments, namely that if managers didn't change their workers' behavior *those managers would be replaced, their workforce would be cut and future benefits would be delayed, if necessary, until pigs fly.* Finally, Neal gave a timeline for these vast and vital improvements in corporate culture to be made— *a whopping two weeks, "Tick, tock."*

Someone within the company (probably one of those parking lot slackers) made Neal's e-mail public and the rest of the world got to see how he treated his employees. Caught in the spotlight, he was quick to admit that his tone, his prescriptions for improvement, and his threats appeared less than "leaderly" to the outside world, but surely his own employees understood what he meant. In fact, "… the memo was taken out of context… most employees at Cerner understood that he exaggerated to make a point." He never intended to carry out any of the punishments he listed. Instead, he said, he sought to promote discussion.

What a savvy way to open the floor to some honest, constructive conversation!

During some deep (yet ultimately self-serving and trite) soul searching, Neal reflected on both his interpersonal insensitivity and the gap between how his messages were intended and how they were received. He could only conclude that his management style came about as a result of his lonely, wheat farm upbringing. "'You can take the boy off the farm,' he said, 'but you can't take the farm out of the boy.'"

That management style had gotten him a long ways thus far. By all standards, Neal's career, first as a consultant with Arthur Andersen, then as a founder of a company valued (at the time) at $1.5 billion, has been a roaring success. His noted arrogance, bluntness of language, personal drive, passion, and vitriol had worked well until then. He relied on that management style up to and through the crisis moment of March 13, 2001, when he decided to drum up his troops.

"That sometimes requires sharp language," he said, "and his employees know how to take it with a grain of salt."

This experience could help Neal grow, but I doubt it. Or maybe it will help other CEOs who read about it change their management style before they run into their own walls… but I doubt that, too. Most of the consultants and analysts quoted in the *New York Times*' article were unanimous in their analysis of the deep error in judgment and leadership Neal committed, one for which all CEOs need to be ever vigilant:

Don't use e-mail!

The CEOs of Big Corporations

Now that we're onto CEOs as an untapped source of appropriate examples for Moron Management behavior… it's time to let even more of them have it.

Where do we start?

Remember when Enron—Wall Street's darling—was such a scandalous shock? How passé! Leaders today are showing their true colors like the latest runway fashion. Consider that in 2003 alone…

Dennis Kozlowski went on trial for his Nero-esque celebrations, fiddling while Tyco burned.

Sam Waksal at ImClone headed to jail… but not before he invited Martha Stewart to share a few stock tips.

HealthSouth's Richard Scrushy found himself facing an 85-count indictment.

Richard Grasso, head of the New York Stock Exchange, after having risen through the ranks from mail boy to CEO, found himself at the pinnacle of success thanks to a compliant board padded with his closest friends. $188 million dollars later, he resigned because of misperceptions about his severance.

Meanwhile, as the economy continues its bumpy ride, CEOs all over the country are getting tough and making the hard decisions: Deep cuts in the workforce, reductions in compensation, and benefits packages, closed plants, offices and factories. These days, that's what needs to be done, and who can blame them? After all, CEOs (according to today's mantra) get paid to serve Shareholders, and Shareholders are taking a mighty big hit.

However, the CEOs keep getting paid more and more.

Performance goals? Compensation tied to results? A bar that gets raised higher every year? All that accountability stuff for which CEOs clamor? That's for chumps.

But why stop with compensation? There are plenty more examples out there of the consequences of interpersonal stupidity.

How about the famous Chainsaw Al Dunlop of Sunbeam fame? He was the first to realize that the quickest (short term) way to turn a company's balance sheet around was to fire as many people as possible at once, thus relieving the company of the burden of all those pay checks. Al got so much compensation for doing this that one has to acknowledge that it was a shrewd move—for him. Of course, he couldn't get a job as CEO of his neighborhood Dog Pound now. Today, the company he "reorganized" is a mere shell of its former self. Nonetheless, other CEOs saw the light and followed his ways, despite the fact that morale was shot, productivity and innovation plummeted, and many of those companies became easy pickings for some other entity. Wall Street got a temporary kick out of it, and the CEOs made off like bandits.

Let's not forget Philip M. Condit, Chairman and CEO of the Boeing Company. Love that leadership. Like so much other incriminating documentation, he tried to take eight decades of tradition and community identity in Seattle and shove it through the paper shredder, suddenly announcing that Boeing would relocate its corporate headquarters to either Chicago, Denver, or Dallas. Not content with merely uprooting the organization, he led a team which incorporated bribery into its contract negotiation strategy. When he was discovered, Condit stepped aside—a little earlier than planned.

Then, there's Jurgen Schrempp, CEO of Daimler, who infamously described his company's $36 billion purchase of Chrysler as a "merger of equals." He then proceeded to isolate all Chrysler senior executives, dictate terms of the new arrangement, alienate its proud workforce, and lower the market value of the combined Daimler-Chrysler. A few years later, under oath, he admitted that he never really considered the merger to be a partnership, but if he'd told the truth, who would have gone along with the idea?

How about the managers at Morton-Thiokol who weren't open enough with their staff or felt safe enough to mention that the Space Shuttle's O-rings were faulty? There's proof positive that Moron Management is *not* rocket science. Or the executives at Ford who pushed forward the development of the SUV over the protests of their engineers and had to spend years catching up in terms of quality and performance. Or the executives at Bridgestone-Firestone who refused to take responsibility for hundreds of deaths caused by their faulty tires…

Flip open the paper; turn on the news. It's all around you. Moron Managers rule the world. In fact, they propagate their rule by selecting as successors other Moron Managers just like them.

How does that make you feel about your last promotion?

Your Chance to Submit to the Academy (www.mybossisamoronmanager.com)

No doubt, out of your own torrid, personal experience in corporate life, you can think of even better examples of Moron Managers who could justifiably take their place in the Hall of Shame. We welcome your nominations and encourage you to submit those profiles and detailed examples to the web page listed above. At the very least, it's healthy to vent, have a laugh, send a message to your boss, or warn future suckers about the danger of their clutches.

Here's the funny twist to all of this… one of my little jokes on you in yet another of its many aggravating forms…

The interpersonal atrocities that we
find most offensive in others
are the things that we are so good at
doing ourselves but fail to realize

How's that, you ask? Now what's this pinhead talking about?

Listen closely… It's easy to see Moron Management behavior in others. It's oh so difficult to see it in ourselves. But the faults we see in others are almost always the very faults we are blind to in ourselves… Let me explain.

We don't notice all the bad things people do; we only notice a fraction. Ever have someone in the office you really hate because he is a _____ (insert offensive behavior-based description here)?

Have you ever found to your amazement that your friends in the office don't notice or aren't bothered by that jerk's atrocious crimes?

The reason why you're particularly bothered that he gets away with it, is because you're likely to be rather skilled at it yourself.

The two or three things we vehemently dislike in others usually creep into our own personal style much more than we would like to admit. That's why we're sensitive to them. If we measure key indicators, we typically find those kinds of double-edged swords. People who evaluate themselves as distrusting towards others, are consistently rated the untrustworthiest by others. Trust is their pressure point. On the reverse, people who trust others tend to be perceived as the most trustworthy.

In other words, are you someone who hates people who talk behind other peoples' backs? Well, that's probably because you do it yourself. Despise a sycophant? I bet you're awfully good at kissing rear! Angered by people who say one thing and do the opposite? Yup, you again. Greedy, short-sighted, and self-centered? *Uhuh.* Always agreeing with the boss? Well, you're the one who's really got her ear, aren't you?

Whatever pushes our buttons most sharply, tends to be the buttons we're good at pushing. Whatever we hate in others, tends to be what's basically wrong with ourselves. The people who hit us at a true visceral level of repulsion, are telling us something about ourselves. In fact, they should be our best friends because they're inadvertently providing us with great information about our own Moron Management ways... If only we could see and accept that knowledge.

The Road to Getting Better (And you without your shoes)

I hope you're getting used to having these painful truths revealed to you. I hope that, as result, you're finally losing some confidence in your skills as a People Person and are no longer strutting around declaring that to be your own unique strategic advantage. Indeed, if you fall far enough in your own esteem, you might stand a chance of becoming the leader you're not.

As it is, I'm fairly certain that you are not a monster... not yet anyway. In fact, you're probably a reasonably decent, fairly accomplished person with good intentions...

But, listen to me now, please.

Although you may have 12 great traits and another 12 terrific attributes, you probably have one or two interpersonal dark spots that will be your undoing, and that's no small matter.

The problem is that we are blind to what those faults are. I've told you why. I've described the many ways in which we fool ourselves, lie to ourselves, or fail to learn from what others are telling us. If you forget those lessons, the guidance I give you in the final section of this book, is not going to help.

You really do want to get better. Maybe you sense your career is on the line. Maybe you just want to feel better in your own skin. Maybe you know your family is getting a raw deal.

Well, I wish I could give you the Girl Scout Badge for "Trying" right now, but I can't. As they say in the Recovery Program Business…

Trying…
is lying.

Meaning… the REAL work is still to come.

Poor you. I know it's been tough so far. But you've got to go further than you even thought possible…

And that, my friend, is very good news.

The Royal Road To Getting REAL
* How To Buy Your Way Out *

- **Attacking others may be your greatest insight.**

  That which you detest in others, be they peers, subordinates, or managers, probably has a home somewhere *within you.* You must accept that and own it before you can neutralize it and overcome it. Examine your "enemies," then appreciate them for the insight!

- **Transforming your epitaph into a eulogy.**

  Sitting in front of that mirror, write your own Hall of Shame Epitaph... and then commit to two specific, observable actions, which will dismantle that epitaph and turn it into a eulogy.

- **Turning intentions into reality.**

  Make a list of your greatest intentions. What are you trying to accomplish as a leader? How would you like to be perceived? How would you wish be remembered? Then, in front of that mirror, catalogue which of your actions and behaviors subvert your intentions. Remember, when changing to become the leader you're not... TRYING IS LYING! The road to REAL leadership is not paved with good intentions.

Step 3

Getting REAL About Change

....

Chapter Six

The Paradox Of Leadership
or
What It Means To
Get REAL

So, who are the REAL leaders? What makes them different from the Moron Managers? How can you tell one from the other?

It's easy. Ask their followers. Although, if you want an honest answer from those who work for a Moron Manager, you might have to promise to enroll them in the Witness Protection Program.

Otherwise, from the outside, the distinctions can be pretty hazy. After all, Moron Managers are very skilled at looking good. In fact, that's their main priority. And so, as a result, they sometimes manage to rise high in the ranks, accumulate prestige and power, and be thought of as paragons of leadership before the lights get turned on and their hideous Mr. Hyde persona is exposed for the rest of us to see.

To help you feel safe when you go to bed tonight, here's a definition to distinguish the leaders in your dreams from the Moron Managers hiding in your closet.

REAL Leaders give
Moron Managers take

That's it in a nutshell. The rest is merely detail.

But don't worry; you'll get your money's worth. I would never let those details go unrevealed.

A leader is deeply concerned about his followers' well-being, even placing it above his own. It's what distinguishes him most from Moron Managers.

A Moron Manager is deeply concerned about his <u>own</u> well-being—although he rarely, if ever, publicly acknowledges such avarice. Instead, he uses others around him to satisfy his self-interest, further his career, solidify his position and make himself look good to the powers-that-be...

Why such a profound difference...?

Because a leader understands that he is powerless alone. He recognizes that he needs the unflagging commitment, true support and unrestrained creative energy of those around him to accomplish virtually anything that matters. He knows that these things must be given freely to be genuinely valuable and inspirational. He further understands that his followers must feel as if they are growing as people in the process.

A Moron Manager actually believes in his own power. He feels that his position entitles him to exert influence over others. The problem is, outside of a prison or military environment, it's not easy to force another human being to do much of anything. A Moron Manager, therefore, usually has to resort to threats or bribes, punishments or perks and other underhanded, short-term, fundamentally manipulative, quid-pro-quo methods to get his way.

A leader knows he can only get by giving. A Moron Manager thinks he only gets what he is able to take.

But how come…?

Because a leader realizes that people must feel looked after, cared for, respected and nurtured to do well. He knows that he could hold a gun to someone's head and get their best efforts for a short period of time, but that technique is not a motivational method designed for longer term success.

Some people learn this and still don't get it. They use caring as just another management tool. True caring, however, is difficult. For a REAL leader, caring is not just a slightly more round-about path to his own ends; it's the <u>best part</u> of the journey. A leader views the people around him as essential contributors, equal collaborators and enthusiastic participants in a grand adventure. He gets as much satisfaction and thrill out of seeing his people grow as he does seeing the adventure, goal, objective or vision succeed.

This is why a leader is hyper-sensitive to how he affects the well-being of the people around him. In fact, because of his position of authority, he believes that he has a disproportionate impact, positive or negative, on people's lives.

This sensitivity does not come naturally for any human being. It's something that a leader works on <u>all the time</u>. Through chronic introspection and nagging self-doubt, a leader exposes himself to the truth of the gaps between his intentions and his actions. He measures his success as a leader by how others view him, not by how he would like to evaluate himself. He takes direct responsibility for the things that go wrong and gives the credit to others for the things that go right.

A Moron Manager, on the other hand, is willfully blind to how he affects the people around him. In fact, he self-protects so well that he is able to inflate how much positive impact he has on others and completely deny the negative. Rather than measure his success by how others view him, a Moron Manager suppresses the negative messages that he is given and never receives any personal benefit as a result. Witness a Moron Manager's typical interpretation of feedback he doesn't like: "My people don't really know me" or "They don't understand the big picture" or "Being a leader means being tough, not being loved," all excuses designed to deflect the truth.

A Moron Manager is capable of doing this because he only cares about how good he looks. He views the people around him as functions or collections of competencies, cogs in the wheel of his own progress. He views them as expendable as soon as they stop producing.

Starting to get the picture?

Not very pretty, I'm sure you'll agree...

Don't Believe Me? (Then, believe them!)

Leadership is tough, never-endingly arduous and all too rare. That's the theme of this chapter, and you'll hear it a couple more times before we're through.

Nevertheless, you're right to wonder what makes it so much harder to be a leader than a Moron Manager. Why are REAL leaders so rare when Moron Managers are so legion? If that's a philosophical question you'd like to have answered, I'm happy to oblige. And here's my answer.

Because it's so "unnatural."

A leader has to work at becoming the leader he's not because he knows that, as human beings, we're hard-wired to think about our own most basic needs first. That's what comes naturally. Self-aggrandizement and self-protection are primary impulses, which is why the self-serving attitude of Moron Management is so common.

I know that you don't want to think that way about yourself and the human race in general. However, I'm not asking you to take my word for it alone. Take a look at the following landmark scientific studies and judge for yourself.

You couldn't make this stuff up if you tried. In fact, it would be funny, if it weren't so sad... and frightening.

The Asch Conformity Study

If you think that it's easy for human beings to lead... think again.

Solomon Asch wanted to test how easy or difficult it was for people to think for themselves. He designed a simple test.

Person after person was brought in to look at a basic line drawing. There were always five or six people in the room, and the target of the experiment, the "subject", was always the fifth or sixth person.

Four lines stacked evenly on top of each other were projected onto the wall. One of the lines was longer than the others. The experimenter asked them to identify which one. No nuclear science exam, this!

To make it interesting, the target of the experiment was asked to answer last. The other four or five participants, who were actually in league with the experimenter, each said that the shortest of the lines was, in fact, the longest.

And what did the target of the experiment say when it came to his turn?

Despite any inclinations to the contrary, he followed right along. "Yup, right you are," he'd say. "That's how I see it, too."

It didn't happen just once. It happened an overwhelming majority of times, across cultures, and educational or economic distinctions. It didn't matter that the correct answer was so clear that even monkeys picked up on it after only a few trials. It didn't matter that the line drawing was not as challenging as nuclear physics or—gulp— management. It didn't matter that it was not a complex or ambiguous situation, nor a test of character or moral fortitude. It was just a series of lines, one of them shorter than the others... and they still got it wrong.

Rather than see the truth and lead the way, the Moron Manager went along with the gang.

The Milgram Obedience Study

If you think it's difficult for human beings to inflict pain and punishment on each other... think again.

Stanley Milgram wanted to study how susceptible people were to obeying authority, especially when that authority encouraged hurtful acts. He designed a morally unambiguous test to see.

The subject of the experiment was cast in the role of "the helper." Before the experiment began, he got to meet a person who he <u>thought</u>

was the target of the experiment—"the learner." This person was hooked up to a machine which was capable of administering painful electric shocks. His own job, he was told, was to help this person learn something through the application of negative reinforcement.

He was asked to join the experimenter in another room and given control over a red shock-generating button and the dial which adjusted the level of the jolt. The experimenter began teaching the person hooked up to the machine various things. When this person made mistakes, the helper was asked to administer a jolt. The effects of that jolt, the sound of the person's sudden pain, could be heard through the wall.

As the experiment continued, the person in the other room kept making mistakes. As the mistakes got worse, the experimenter gently encouraged the helper to increase the voltage. The dial had only three ranges of settings, one green range, one blue range, one red range. As the red "danger" zone was reached and high level shocks were administered the person in the other room would scream in horrible pain, begging for the experiment to stop.

Did the helper step back from his instructions and say, "Wait a minute. This is crazy. This person is in serious pain!"?

Nope.

In the overwhelming majority of cases, people were willing, if not eager, to administer painful, seemingly life-threatening jolts of electricity at the mild instructions of others. They never questioned what they were doing.

Shortly before his death, Stanley Milgram was asked by Morley Safer on 60 Minutes what he'd learned over 25 years of conducting this, his most famous of experiments. Stanley casually, yet despondently replied, "…if a system of death camps were set up in the United States of the sort we had seen in Nazi Germany, one would be able to find sufficient personnel for those camps in any medium-sized American city."

No doubt, Moron Managers would amply fill those ranks.

The Stanford Prison Study

If you think it's easy for human beings to resist abusing power...
think again.

Philip Zimbardo and a team of social psychologists at Stanford wanted to test how susceptible people were to assuming a role. They created a situation in which the differentiation of roles was as clear-cut as it could be.

Fifty male students, between the ages of 19 and 23—all smart enough to get into Stanford, all "personality tested" in advance to make sure they did not have any mental health issues—volunteered and were selected to be part of a study. They did not know what the study entailed nor when it would begin. A month later, however, "police" showed up at the various dorm rooms on campus, rounded up all the selected participants, blindfolded them and brought them to the site of the experiment.

In the basement of the Psychology Building, a mock prison had been built. Randomly, half the subjects were told that they had been arrested and were now prisoners. The other half were told that they were assigned to serve as guards. The experimenters let the "prisoner" and "guard" populations interact without interference or direction and watched to see what would happen.

The experiment was scheduled to run 7 days. After 48 hours, it needed to be terminated because the level of aggression inflicted by the "guards" on the "prisoners" was too severe to continue.

What kinds of things did those "guards" do?

Without any prompting or outside influence, they took away prisoners' clothes to emasculate them, split them into subgroups of informers and traitors to humiliate them, engaged in physical and emotional abuse to degrade them, and withheld food and bathroom privileges to punish them… all within the first six hours.

During later debriefing, some common feelings emerged. The essential one was this: After about 5 hours, people could no longer claim that they were simply playing a role anymore. It didn't matter if they had been assigned as a prisoner or a guard…

The experimenters believed that the results showed two things: Assuming a role allows a person great liberty with regard to what they become capable of doing; those roles carry with them certain norms which we find nearly impossible to resist… and eventually embrace. Situational contexts have a clear and powerful effect on how we choose to behave, and Moran Managers have become expert at internalizing those norms!

Think about that the next time you contemplate your organization's succession plan.

The Pygmalion Study

Finally, if you think it's difficult for human beings in authority positions to affect other's performance and behavior… think again.

Robert Rosenthal at Harvard University wanted to see how accurately our perceptions of people match with their abilities and how those expectations affect the way we then evaluate them. He created a situation in which people in authority were given a glimpse of the ability of those in their charge and analyzed the results.

At the beginning of the school year, Rosenthal administered a battery of IQ tests to the entire 3rd grade of five Boston Public Elementary Schools.

After the results were calculated, Rosenthal sat with the teachers of each class to let them know the IQ make-up of their students. Those with the highest IQ's, Rosenthal said, pointing to the names of one third of the students, were going to contribute as great students. Those with average IQ's, Rosenthal said, pointing to the names of another one third of the students, were going to do okay. And those with lower IQ's, Rosenthal said, pointing to the names of the final third of the students, were intellectually inferior and likely to be the biggest trouble makers and poorest producers.

Then he went away.

After the school year was over, Rosenthal correlated report cards with the way students' IQ's had been ranked. He found that they were a perfect match. Students identified as smart got high marks and positive accolades. The middle group got average grades, some of them having exhibited behavior problems. The lower ranked group did poorly across the board, causing many to be held back.

The results were unremarkable, except for one minor detail: After administering the IQ tests, Rosenthal had ignored the test results and assigned students randomly to each of the three groups.

It's clear, Rosenthal concluded, that our expectations shape performance. He was making a point about race... but he could have been talking about management systems. Moron Managers are not unlike those 3rd grade teachers. They fail to grasp how resolutely they shape the performance of their people while assuming no blame for the results.

So, what do you think of them apples? Here are the things that all of those studies showed a majority of people being unable to do:

- Think for themselves in group situations, despite direct evidence that everyone else is wrong.
- Refrain from inflicting cruel punishment on people when mildly encouraged to do so, even when cast in the ostensible role of "helper."

- Remain sensitive to the feelings of others when cast in the role of the powerful.
- Be conscious of how much those in a position of authority affect the way people perform and behave.

A leader, somehow, avoids all of those natural inclinations and traps. He...

- Acknowledges, and stands up for, the truth that others refuse to see.
- Genuinely cares for the people he is assigned to help and acts in their best interest.
- Resists assuming the norms of power.
- Is hyper-vigilant about how he affects the feelings and performance of the people around him.

If you want to become someone who can do all that, you're going to have to be brutally honest with yourself and work at it all the time. I hope you didn't expect that leadership was going to be easy.

What Leaders "Do" (That managers "don't")

Internal forces drive what a person does, a Moron Manager no less than a leader. We've learned, however, that we can't judge another person's intentions, we can only evaluate their actions. So, let's get down to the hard evidence of behaviors.

What is it that leaders "do" that managers "don't"?

Leaders are "REAL" with their followers. It's what they do and how they act.

Let's review. Getting REAL means being and living...

Responsible (for self & others)
Empowered (in self & in others)
Accountable, and (to self & others)
Loving (towards self & others)

These are not just feelings; they are behaviors that generate emotions and responses in others. Let's look at them, one at a time.

Feel & Get RESPONSIBLE

A leader knows that there is only one difference between the supervisor and the supervised. As supervisor, a person knowingly, willingly and intentionally accepts responsibility for the outcomes generated by others.

A leader acts as if he is responsible for those outcomes and more. He knows that he impacts his followers' sense of well-being and the way they are able to channel their energies in contributing to their output.

If you think I'm saying that being a leader means being soft, then you're misreading this book. A leader sets the highest of standards for himself and others. Even though a leader is extremely demanding, he feels responsible for making sure that people can fill those demands and meet those standards.

A leader makes the hard decisions. But even though a leader is able to fire someone who can't or won't contribute, he feels responsible for the reasons why and makes sure that the act of firing is at the very least an enlightening and educational experience for all involved, and preferably a positive one.

A leader is relentless about the truth. But even though a leader won't allow others—much less himself—to hide behind excuses, he never uses that as a way of excusing himself if things go wrong.

Here's what you can do to begin to Get RESPONSIBLE:

- Act as if you are responsible, not just for yourself and your contribution, but for others and their contributions as well.
- Own others' well-being and level of motivation. After all, you helped create it, good or bad. Feelings do matter; treat them as though they do.
- Sanctify your own emotional well-being as critical for your success because how YOU feel is critical for their success.
- Constantly pay attention to how you affect others, including how they really see you, what they say behind your back and what they would like to say to your face. Own these perceptions.
- Repeat after me, "The soft stuff is the hard stuff…" Repeat after me, "The soft stuff is the hard stuff…"

Get EMPOWERED & Be EMPOWERING

Getting empowered also works two ways. A leader drives himself to be empowered and encourages others to be empowered in turn. That's because a leader doesn't share power, he gives it away, freely and copiously, knowing that the more he gives, the more he gets.

A leader understands that individuals are instrumental in the cause of things, that people make things happen, not corporations, governments, or societies. Accordingly, a leader knows that he must take action, no matter how risky or threatening it is to do so, because others are waiting to follow someone who does.

A leader does not view himself as a failure or in need of punishment if his actions do not succeed. It's never wrong to try.

On the opposite side of the coin, a leader encourages the empowerment of others because he does not view the people around him as a source of threat, but as a source of strength, opportunity and enhancement.

It's a difficult notion to accept. We're taught that power needs to be hoarded and conserved or else it dissipates... but the opposite is true. A leader knows that the best thing he can do is outline the big picture and let his followers provide the details, by expressing themselves to their fullest with the freedom to act as they see fit.

A leader does not correct, punish or chastise when people color outside the lines or make "mistakes." Instead, a leader seizes every opportunity as a teachable moment to figure out together, in a supportive way, the best approach and solution.

Does this sound parental? It should. And what's wrong with that? Take a look at the dynamic forces at the heart of the manager-subordinate relationship. Power. Dependency. Direction. Recognition. Sound familiar? It's parenthood all over again, although few of us exploit that for our betterment. A leader recognizes that those four basic ingredients are a potent mix for breeding passion, focus and commitment and for teaching new ways.

Here's what you can do to begin to Get EMPOWERED yourself and encourage Empowerment in others:

- Understand that no one is going to empower you or anyone else.
- Know that the core of empowerment is courage, know that you have options, know that YOU must be the one to act, "If it is to be, it's up to me".
- Always remember that you need them more than they need you!
- Act as if you're a volunteer, not an indentured servant.
- Question authority, always—but do it to their faces!
- Say "No" to meaningless tasks.
- Set meaningful goals for your followers, not menial tasks.
- Give power away—it always comes back twofold!
- Ask your colleagues what you do that disempowers them... then stop it!

Get ACCOUNTABLE & Hold Others ACCOUNTABLE

A leader sees what needs to be done or questions the <u>current state</u> of things in order to determine what <u>should be</u> done. This is the driving force behind his need to promote change and improvement. He feels accountable for the state of his world because he knows he can and should do something to better it.

A leader also feels accountable for his own actions. He understands that everything he does has consequences (remember the Rosenthal experiments). This is a breakthrough in thinking that most of us can't even imagine.

A leader recognizes that the way he treats people impacts how they feel. That is why a leader is hyper-sensitive to how what he does is interpreted by others. He knows, however, that he can't possibly interpret how others feel about what he does… not without their honest feedback. That is why he considers the way people feel about what he does to be his ultimate yardstick.

Here's what you can do to begin to Get Accountable:

- Understand that what you do matters, really matters… if it doesn't, don't do it.
- Know that your every breathing act affects those around you. Because of that, you are "under a constant microscope" being observed and evaluated for evidence of one thing: "Is this leader worth following?"
- Define yourself as the "causal agent" within your team, group or organization.
- Let your impact on others be your yardstick—even if you're firing someone.
- Act as if <u>how</u> you do things creates an indelible impression. You are

using magic markers on the wall, not water colors on a white board.

Feel and Get LOVING

Being Loving is the lynchpin for all the other behaviors in the Get REAL model. It is the reason why the efforts that go into getting better at being Responsible, Empowered and Accountable are always genuine and not something done to perfect a "leadership technique."

Loving is not a concept that many of us are comfortable talking about, especially in a business setting. Too bad. Do you think that human beings should devote their lives towards anything less? It's a shame that we water down this concept into insipid management techniques like "rewards and recognition" or "positive reinforcement," all hollow and safe approximations of what we all really want.

Leaders demonstrate loving first of all because they love what they are doing. This is the source of their energy, optimism, and stamina. It is why they are committed to giving as much effort, care, attention, creativity and faith as it takes to succeed. Why do they love what they are doing? Because they see that work as an expression of who they are, the path towards becoming who they want or need to be.

Leaders also love those with whom they work, spawning feelings of nurturing, caring, compassion, concern, responsibility, accountability and empowerment for others. Why would that happen? Because Leaders see others as contributing so much of themselves in the cause of the leader's vision… in the process becoming someone better than before… creating something more and better for everyone.

Here's what you can do to begin to Get Loving:

- Love what you do and those who work with you. Let them know it… regularly and openly.
- Pretend you work with volunteers and treat them accordingly.

- Openly demonstrate affection, concern and caring for the people you work with, not just their utility contributions. Tell them how you feel.
- Acknowledge, accept and embrace the power of love as a motivational source in your work.
- Express yourself with positive emotions. Don't equate being honest with being mean and demoralizing, as most Moron Managers do.
- Ask your people what they really need… and take care of yourself, too. Tell your people and your own manager what you really need.

The Hall Of REAL Leaders
(Close your eyes & step right in.)

Are your eyes still closed? Good, keep them that way for the moment.

It's time to put my money where my mouth is. I've been describing Moron Managers for over a hundred pages now… even providing you with detailed portraits of a half dozen people who exhibit Moron Management traits (unfortunately) well. No doubt, you are parched for some good news by this point. It's not surprising. We all like to look up to leaders, admire what they do, and wonder how they impact the world. We'd like to emulate them in our own way, or at least, imagine that we can. There's something about a great leader that ennobles the rest of us… and that's no small thing.

So, as a tonic, a remedy, a refresher, a counterbalance to all of the negative examples I've provided you with thus far, prepare for your reward… hold your impatience just a moment longer, step right in to the Hall of REAL Leaders… and… open… your… eyes…

EMPTY

Sorry to disappoint.

Did you think that becoming the leader you're not would be that easy?

...would be that easy?

...that easy?

...easy?

...sy?

Ooops. Excuse the echo. It sure is cavernous in here.

I was tempted to provide you with actual examples, believe me, if for no other reason than to prove to you that I know that of which I write. I would dearly love to describe the Naval Commander who empowered everyone on his ship to be creative and independent-minded despite hundreds of years of military tradition to the contrary ... or the head of sales at a major distributor who bought a thousand roses for everyone on his staff to express to them how much he cared... or the corporate vice president at one of the world's top three revenue generating companies who transformed himself from world-class asshole to world-class listener... or the professional coach who manages emotional states of mind first and foremost and lets the performance of his star athletes fall into place as a result... or the corporate nurse who for forty years badgered and chastised everyone from part-time workers to regional managers to QUIT SMOKING (to great effect) and whose retirement party was attended by the hundreds of people whose lives she touched and probably extended.

But I don't want to talk about them.

I want to talk about you.

Leaders are not profound or saintly. I think it's important not to hold anyone up as a simplistic example of Leader—because no one is a leader all the time or in all aspects of their life. Not so far as I am aware.

Leaders engage in leaderly activity in certain arenas or circumstances over things that mean something to them. We should be aware that they may fail us miserably if we wait for them to be leaderly in every aspect of their lives, indiscriminately.

So, don't look to other leaders for the answers... just look to yourself.

You are not going to become the leader you're not by emulating others whose lives you admire. I understand the urge. I do it myself. But just because you watch what they do doesn't mean that you can change in ways that make you able to copy them...

You are not going to become the leader you're not by following my prescriptive advice, either. I'm providing it anyway because, hey, it's a book. I'm being as spare and simple as I can because I know that <u>you</u> have to fill in the details.

The only way you are going to become the leader you're not is by growing in awareness of what you need to do <u>internally</u>. You need to change who you are now in order to become who you need to be.

Although I have proven that what you do is negative and shown how hard the change you seek will be, I can't describe to <u>you</u> what you need to become, except in the broadest terms. Only <u>you</u> can know what <u>you</u> believe and feel and what matters most to you... even though you might not, yet.

What I can tell you is that <u>you</u> can become the leader you're not, should you choose to put in the effort, the attention and the deliberate thoughtfulness. Also, I can tell you that you don't have to be great to be good. This process, after all, is never-ending. You are not going to become a Great Leader over night, in the historical sense, nor may you ever have the luck or misfortune to be part of the kind of circumstances that might permit you to try.

There is, however, tremendous value in doing this because there is so much more that you can be. Everyone can't be great... but everyone can get better... and in their way, make their world and the people in it better as a result. You do not need to be the smartest person with the most talent, or be the best looking or the most charismatic. All of those things are mere attributes compared to the power of knowing what matters to you and the payoff of working hard to understand what others feel.

Leadership is a state of mind... and so is Moron Management. Moron Management is a series of skills designed to let you off the hook, provide you with excuses, give you an easy out. Being a leader is tough—but it is infinitely more satisfying and fulfilling on a personal level and much more productive and effective on a social level.

It's up to you to decide whether you want to make the effort to become a leader or remain a Moron Manager.

I can't promise you how far you'll get or how much you'll get out of it. However, if you decide to take the Leadership path, you will be better tomorrow than you are today...

That's the only guarantee you'll ever get from me.

The Royal Road To Getting REAL
* On Your Way To Recovery *

- ## Become the Leader you're not....
  When giving who you "are" to others, give who you "want to be" instead. Who you are isn't good enough anymore. You're no different than those around you, except for the title. The moment that you think you are special is the day your descent begins. Remember... humility... *not* hubris!

- ## True self-awareness is anything but self-indulgent.
  Be ever-vigilant about the effect you have on those around you; "ever-vigilant" is not paranoia, since it stems from a core of caring.

- ## Efficiency does not equal effectiveness.
  Changing yourself is a long journey that takes hard work. After all, it took you (fill in your age) years to get the way you are now! The good news is you can begin the journey now; the bad news is, you'll never finish.

Chapter Seven

....

Lobotomy or Transplant?
or
A Radical Choice For REAL Results...But What Choice Have You Got?

So, what's it going to be? Shall we push on to the stage in which you become a REAL leader?

"Sure!" you say. "I'm gung-ho to get all fixed up. Shouldn't be too hard!"

Oh?

Let me tell you a story.

I had a client who said that to me once. We were talking about the fairly substantial things that he needed to do differently in order to begin becoming the leader he wasn't. I said things to him like:

- You need to learn how to get people to trust you
- You need to make people understand that you respect them
- You need to be able to open up about how you genuinely feel towards others

And after about 30 minutes of me knocking the stuffing out of who he was and laying out how truly far he had to go to become someone different, he said...

"Well, that shouldn't be too hard!"

It took me a few minutes to recover. I seethed to the point that I thought that I would explode. But I was also very, very impressed.

Human beings, I thought to myself, have an amazing energy, a nearly limitless, passive-aggressive capacity for being completely out of touch with how difficult it is to become better. It's a testament to something wondrous and awe inspiring, though I'm not sure what.

So, after I managed to get myself under control, I said to that person what I am about to say to you. I asked him to sit back, close his eyes, and try Leadership Exercise #1.

Leadership Exercise #1
(Do not try at home without a net.)

First, I recommend that you wear loose clothes. I also suggest you put on a helmet, since I can't be responsible for any physical injuries you cause yourself. Finally, I suggest you put on sunglasses, a little sun screen on the bridge of your nose, a long sleeve shirt and a pair of leather gloves, since there's a chance the blinding flash of insight you are about to receive might cause scorch marks.

Found a chair? Sitting down? Ready?

Not quite? What's wrong?… Are you scared?

You should be.

Here we go.

Cross your arms.

Yes. That's the exercise. Cross your arms. Don't be shy. Just go ahead and do it. Got it? Good. Congratulations. You've passed part one of the test. You've shown me who you really are in your "natural" state.

Ready for part two?

I've noticed that your right arm is over your left. I want you to reverse them.

That's right. Your right arm… lift it away from your left arm… you do remember left from right, don't you? Oh, you had to think about it for a moment? Fine, now cross them again with the left one… yes, that's the left one… over… the right one…

Got it?

I bet you're feeling a little strange all of a sudden. Off-balance… uncertain… out of sorts… awkward… different.

If I was leading that exercise in an auditorium full of senior executives from Fortune 500 companies, half of them would have fallen off their chairs by now.

My point is, crossing your arms the other way doesn't feel very natural, does it?

And you thought changing your personality was going to be easy.

Well, the good news is, I can teach you how to become expert at the reverse arm cross. Just do it fifty times a day, every day for a year. If you're lucky, it might start feeling natural in time for your next birthday.

There you go, your birthday gift to yourself. You get to feel like a brand new person.

"Daddy, Are You Dying?"
(And other Country & Western hits on
Moron Management Easy Listening Radio)

Awkward. You know that feeling you get when you do something different…

Get used to it. You'll learn to love it. In fact, the Power of Awkward is the only tool you'll ever really need.

The fact is you never learn anything new by being comfortable. And you've been comfortable for a long, long time. I bet you even sit on the same part of the couch every night that you watch TV, don't you? Do me a favor. Get up and try a new chair, right now. The entire world looks different, doesn't it? You probably never really noticed that wall before now. Your spouse looks taller than normal. The picture frame, it turns out, has been crooked for years. And what's that strange feeling? Ah, yes, the new seat just doesn't seem right under the old rear end.

Well, just think about how other parts of your anatomy—like your brain—are going to feel soon.

No one provides us with developmental guidance in being a better person. As a result, we end up doing what feels "right" to us. We might be able to see that what we do is "wrong" for others, but we're equally good at exonerating our failings and subverting our need for change. That's what Moron Managers say all the time, isn't it? "That's just who I am" or "I can't do anything to change."

The way we relate to others. The way we treat people "below" us. The amount of trust or empathy we have. How much we're willing to do for another person, how much we believe in them, how much we will share with them.

We've all got our own personal standards for what feels right. How we developed those standards, typically, is through our early family experiences.

Now, let's pause for a moment to reflect on the dynamics of our own happy upbringing… After all, didn't Tolstoy say something such as all unhappy families are alike, every happy family is unique in its own way…

Or was it the other way around? Come to think of it, I don't think the "We're Such A Wonderfully Happy Family" story ever made it into an 800 page novel, did it?

Most of us do what feels right because that's where we learned what "right" feels like… at home with our parents and siblings.

It's a fairly horrifying thought, isn't it? Remember that dinner table? The hierarchy of command in the TV room? The way chores were delegated, recognized, and rewarded? How openly and support-ively issues, underlying tensions or ideas were discussed? If you've for-gotten what it was like, spend a weekend with your parents and sib-lings again. Let the rest of us know how much time elapses before the whole happy gang of you reverts back to those old habits.

Now, think about that last meeting you conducted.

That's why change is so hard. The first time you do something that is not "who you are" is going to feel very awkward. Remember riding that bike without training wheels? How about the first time you turned on a computer? Or even the first day you called an adult in a formal setting by their first name?

None of those times felt normal or right or "who you are," but you got used to them.

The problem is the <u>interpersonal</u> change I am talking about goes a bit deeper than that. You've been handling relationships more or less the same way since you were a child, and it's not going to feel very much "like you" when you begin to change that.

Think of water dripping onto rock over many, many years. It starts to get very comfortable running along the same groove.

They say that practice makes perfect, but I've got news for you... it doesn't.

Practice Makes Permanent

Don't believe me? Think of how much practice you've had over the years being a Moron Manager. That's right... you're not perfect... just ask your people! But here's the good news.

You <u>can</u> change. It's going to feel awkward. Something you mistakenly associate with being "un-leaderly." And that feeling of awkward will probably also make you feel:

- Silly
- Stupid
- Ridiculous
- Embarrassed
- Inadequate
- Insecure
- Unnatural, and, of course,
- "Not who you are"

Who among us seeks out, relishes, and embraces situations which induce those feelings? Leaders do. You can, too. Sure it won't be much fun at first, but that doesn't mean you don't have to try. No one said it was going to be easy becoming the leader you're not. That doesn't mean you don't have to do it anyway.

For example...

The first time you tell one of your employees that you like them, they're going to laugh in your face.

Why shouldn't they? You flubbed your lines, your mouth was probably contorted, and your hair was mussed from staying up all night dreading the big moment.

But you've read this book so you know practice makes permanent. As a result, you do it again and again because you know that's the only way to turn the awkward feeling into a natural one, transforming your very personality in the process.

Presto! Chango!

You have become the leader you're not.

In truth, it's not quite that easy. You, my friend, have got a long, long way to go. Don't believe me? Let me tell you a story.

Once upon a time, I set off to conduct group sessions throughout the Northeast for a multi-billion dollar, multi-national trucking company. The audience was filled with drivers, mechanics and supervisors in vests, and black leather jackets, with tattoos, bandanas, baseball caps, rolled up shirts and beer guts.

Enter me... to speak about interpersonal change...

Talk about feeling awkward.

One guy in the group started arguing with my premise, that it was truly difficult to change and become a better person. He assured me that he was good enough already and none of this being better stuff had anything to do with him. So I said, "Okay, I want you to do something for me tonight. We'll even lay a bet on it."

He was so confident and eager to prove me wrong, he agreed before knowing what I wanted him to do.

I told him that all he had to do was to go home that night, gather his two children in the living room and tell each of them in turn that he loved them and was proud of them for being who they are. Then, I added, "When we get together again, you have to tell us what happened." Piece of cake.

The next day he was late.

The session was through the first coffee break when Jim finally snuck into the room.

I spotted him and stopped what we were talking about to ask him to report on what had happened at home.

"I told them I loved them and that I was proud of them," he barked, as if there was nothing more to say.

I asked him to go into a tad more detail.

He said that after dinner he called them into the family room, turned off the TV, and told them.

"Told them what?" I asked.

"Told 'em I loved 'em."

"And?" I said.

"And, that's it."

"But how did they react? What did they say to you?" I asked.

He said, "My son asked me if Mommy and Daddy were getting divorced."

Everyone in the room laughed.

"And?" I asked. "What did your daughter say?"

He paused, gulped, stared into my face like a two year old Buck with a tremendous set of antlers who sees the hunter's gun pointed right at him:

"She asked if I was dying."

The room exploded into whoops.

Managers are always telling me how they reinforce, praise, and let their people know how much they are appreciated. It's so memorable that their employees can usually recall the exact day it happened... ten years ago.

The day you begin to change, your employees are going to look at you with the same kind of suspicion as my trucking company friend's children did to him. Your incompetence at interpersonal relations will make people suspect. The day you start treating "your people" like decent human beings, they'll assume you must be leaving the company, taking a new drug, having an affair, about to be fired, or are about to die.

But that's not enough. To understand the true meaning of awkward, you have to go further. It's challenging to behave "out of character," but the kind of change I'm talking about is more significant and requires more from you. I'm not talking merely about what you do and how you act, although that is critical. I'm talking about who you are, how you look at things and even how you feel… the essence of who you think you are.

Have you ever lived in another country… one that has a completely different culture and language… a place where you don't recognize the food… can't ask for directions… can't read a newspaper or understand what people are saying to you? A place where you're a child all over again?

That's how confusing and helpless you need to feel; born into this world again as a new person… the leader you're not.

Lobotomy or Transplant
(And other remedies for curing who you are)

There are parts of you that you're going to have to cut out, almost surgically—toxic, misery-making aspects of your personality that make you the Moron Manager you are.

That's the lobotomy.

There are parts of you that you're going to have to replace altogether with something different, something not you, something that makes you the Leader You're Not.

That's the transplant.

Both are radical choices… but what choice have you got?

In order to discover which aspects of yourself need to be completely blown up versus which just need to be adjusted, you need to be willing to put yourself under a microscope for an extended period of time. That's the only way you'll have a chance to learn what it is you consistently do that doesn't help the people around you get what they really need and want.

However, putting yourself under a microscope is not likely to be something you can do all by your lonesome… certainly not at first. So here's how I recommend going about it.

Ask Others For Help

Brilliant, aren't I? Will my flashes of wisdom never cease?

You've heard of 360° Feedback? It's a relatively new "intervention" that's all the rage with our friends in Human Resources—probably because it lets other people do the dirty work in a safe, unthreatening way. I recommend trying a version of it.

In a standard 360 Feedback Assessment, a manager will identify a total of five people who work for him, with him and over him. He then asks them to fill out an anonymous report rating his abilities as manager. Once the compiled data is ready, he goes over it with a Human Resources representative to help him interpret the findings. Together they set his future developmental goals, the aim of which is to turn those 3s into 5s. After the cheerful representative from HR has left the room, the Moron Manager takes the entire file, dumps it into the trashcan and goes about behaving, acting and managing as he always has until next year.

And why not? No supervisors get access to that information. No compensation is tied to it. No one gets fired if improvements are not made.

If, on the other hand, you want to really find out what your people think of you, try this. Take the idea of 360° Feedback and make it REAL. I don't mean by exposing yourself to financial or career risk by tying your bonus to the results... although that certainly wouldn't hurt... but by exposing yourself to personal risks. Gather your assessors together in one room at one time and talk to them.

Tell them you sincerely need their help to get better and ask them to talk (without holding anything back) about what it is you do to others that needs to change.

Oh, and don't forget to wear loose clothes, fresh underwear, sunscreen, and all that protective gear again.

It will start slowly, probably. But then the first pebble will slip, a seemingly benign remark about your rudeness perhaps, a sign of the tumult to come. Before long the others will join in and the whole mountain of you will begin to crumble in an avalanche of boulders, trees, clouds of dust and senseless noise.

That's your life beginning to change.

Remember, these people you gather together can see what you can't, stuff that you have made yourself blind to for years. I should warn you that you will not accept their insights easily or readily. In fact, the closer to the mark a comment is, the more it might set off your most defensive reactions—denial, anger, disbelief, dismissal, and aggression. It should hurt so good.

Don't forget why you're doing this, to understand how to get better. You can't do it alone. You need help, and you can't "get better" without knowing the answer to one question: "better than what?" So, be grateful for their openness and honesty, no matter how painful; they're telling you what you need to know.

In return, sit there and take it. Do your best to absorb and understand it. Strive to make the information useful by slowly becoming able to observe it in yourself and perhaps even learn how to change.

One of the ironies of leadership will become apparent here. By setting yourself up as someone who needs help, you'll be showing how strong you really are. By hearing what others really dislike about you... you'll be growing closer to them, not further apart. You won't all hate each other as a result of the blood letting. These people can't help but be on your side now that they know that you want to change. They might even begin to see you as someone worth following because you have the courage and compassion to become better.

They're your future allies... committed to helping you, if you are sincere about changing.

They may even end up respecting and admiring you...

Or even becoming... your followers.

And don't let it stop there.

The analysis of who you are must be undertaken on an ongoing basis. The 360° Avalanche is only a kick start for your new vigilance of self-awareness.

Eventually, through your sincere efforts to uncover the truth of who you and how you affect others, this is what you're going to find needs to be done:

You are going to have to let go of what you think has made you REAL so far. That won't be easy. You've become comfortable doing things to others that are hurtful, counterproductive, and destructive. But the truth is, those activities come from aspects of yourself that you think are intrinsically you... and cutting them out is no simple endeavor.

That's not even the hard part.

Letting go of who you are is one thing... but letting go of your reasons for not doing the things that you should be doing is even harder.

I'm talking about the embarrassment you feel when you say

something kind to someone.

You need to learn how to let it go.

The anxiety you feel when admitting that you don't really know something.

Let that go, too.

The threat you feel when someone questions your authority by asking the simple question, "Why?"

That's right. Let it go.

The desire you feel to get ahead in your career at the expense of others.

You got it. Let it go.

The need you feel to get praise from your superiors for work that "your people" actually did.

Let... it... go!

So the question of lobotomy or transplant is actually two-fold... and you, my friend, need both components. You need to:

- Overcome your personal fears or anxieties about not doing certain things, and...
- Consciously do other things in very different ways...

The Magic Bullet of Leadership
(Just watch where you point that gun.)

How, you wonder, can you take the steps necessary to make yourself over in such a total way?

Where do you start?

The first answer that comes to mind is where shouldn't you start? But, upon reflection, I have a more prescriptive response.

The steps you need to take to become the Leader You're Not will be found in the next chapter. Before that, we need to discuss the surgical procedures necessary for recovering from those Moron Manager tendencies.

Warning: Some of these procedures will strike you as intensely counter-intuitive. In other words, they'll scare the jeepers out of you. And they should!

#1 Diagnose Your Smug Personal Complacency

The first rule in getting better is to acknowledge your illness and decide on a course of treatment. You think you're in the best of health, that your interpersonal skills are strong and vital, that "your people" actually follow you because they choose to rather than because they are biding time until they can get the hell away from you in the least damaging way possible.

In your case, the doctor would like you to understand that:
- You are a Moron Manager.
- You have tremendous, toxic weaknesses that you are able to ignore but others see and are affected by.
- You still think you do not have any weaknesses or create a negative impact on those around you. In other words, your smug complacency is in truly advanced stages... see above.

Your treatment options are...

- To improve your "hard" skills in financial planning, strategic thinking or "management" by reading a book, getting an MBA, or signing up for a new executive education program.
- To retool your "soft" skills by participating in an Outward Bound style team-building retreat, attending a Senior Executive "leadership" summit or reading yet another "communications" Book.

- To change your entire personality—meaning the way you think about others, feel about yourself and how you act—by examining your interpersonal weaknesses closely and taking the deliberate steps necessary to become a genuinely decent human being.

Hint: The courses of action described in A and B are bound to anesthetize the pain while doing nothing to save the patient.

#2 Rein In Self-Interest

Talk about a lobotomy. All corporate America should immediately proceed to pre-op to have their heads shaved.

Some will tell you, business is built on self-interest. "Greed," as Gordon Gecko, that cinematic icon of destruction for short-term benefit, once said, "is good." CEOs certainly demonstrate it every chance they get. Most managers are raised on the model that selfishness makes sense. Indeed, getting the most you can in the quickest fashion for the least amount of effort is just smart business. Compensation systems encourage and reward it, and senior executives pander to those who achieve it. So, who can blame you for doing the same thing?

Your people can and will. And rightfully so.

Leaders know that anyone can look good for a few quarters or a year. Short-term payoffs are as easy as pie. A Moron Manager can walk into a new department, slash jobs, cut costs, abandon old strategies embark on new ones and turn the numbers around quickly. But will it stick? And will anyone be around at the end with the spirit, enthusiasm, brains, and will to continue the job and keep bringing in the numbers? That's a test for you. Are you brave enough to take it? REAL relationships and meaningful change cannot be built around short-term self-interest. Hang around a bit longer than a year and you will reap the fruits of what you have sown.

The leap from manager to leader requires cutting out your pervasive focus on self-interest. It's not easy. The opportunities for abject self-interest are enhanced as a manager rises in the ranks. It doesn't help that they keep throwing stuff your way. Nicer office space. More people. Basketball tickets. Bigger bucks. Love those stock options! All are seductive enticements for you to abandon your concern for others and focus on yourself. Even if you think those things are not important and don't sway your heart, just wait... they'll find something you really want someday and you'll trip all over yourself (and your people) in your eagerness to get it. After all, you deserve it, or someone else will get it... you have to think of your family—insert your own rationalization here.

The motive of self-interest is at the core of all your self-aggrandizement, denial, and suppression. It's what causes others to distrust you, derail you, and abandon you. If you don't believe me, ask 10 business people at random what's the first thing they look up in any annual report, 10K filing, or quarterly statement? Yep, the same thing you do... the salaries, bonuses, stock options, and perks being doled out at others' expense.

True leaders, on the other hand, are able to place the needs of others above their own. Paradoxically, in so doing, they get their own needs met more than they would in any other way.

Have your eyes just lit up? Did you spot an easy way out? You've probably leapt to the conclusion that leaders use self-interest as a kind of tool, delaying it long enough to get what they really want—and with a bigger payoff! If so, you've missed the point. You, my friend, have inadvertently morphed yourself into an "enlightened" Moron Manager—a new breed for our new times and perhaps the most dangerous, manipulative, slimy breed of all.

#3 Transfuse Mental Laziness

Which brings us to our next procedure. Blockages in your internal value systems have caused a lack of blood flow to the actively "critical" parts of your brain. You need an immediate, invigorating transfusion to get rid of the mental laziness which is holding back your recovery.

I'm talking about hard work. Critical thinking. Intensive self-reflection. Open-minded reality checks. A humble, but optimistic, searching for basic truths… a series of mental and interpersonal stretches, contortions, balances, and muscular exertions designed to slowly develop your flexibility, emotional resiliency, compassion, courage, and humor.

You won't be a fully accredited yogi from the very first day you start trying. In fact, in the early days, you'll be lucky if you can touch your toes without ending up in traction.

Making yourself better—for you and for others—is a serious and ongoing challenge. Still, because you are mentally lazy, you are going to want it to be easy and simple… the proverbial quick fix promised by "re-engineering," "managing by objectives" and "executive charm school."

Some of you are going to see the path as getting easier over time. If you *find* that to be the case, it doesn't mean that you're getting better—it simply means you've learned how to fool yourself in entirely new ways.

> *Remember: A leader is always becoming. He never gets there. New challenges will always arise, trickier and less obvious than the earlier ones. That's why mental laziness is such a terrible and insidious defect.*

Others of you are going to want your personal change to be simple. It is… but it's not simplistic. Some of you will try to make it simplistic by being as hard on yourself as possible, changing everything about you in meaningless ways. One executive I know thought that painting his office blue and dying his hair a reddish-brown would change substantially his leadership impact. Others of you will focus on only one major and particularly noxious aspect of yourself, and lose sight of all the little ways that contribute just as negatively. I'm afraid the answer is not a one-way street with a big sign pointing you in the right direction. The solutions are not black and white.

There are going to be certain things about you that you will need to say, "This will never change... and shouldn't," core values, transferable to any circumstances. There are going to be other things you need to revise slightly, good intentions with bad expressions, old habits gone sour because they are out of date. And there are going to be still other things that need to be annihilated entirely, those cruel practices you enjoy so much and rationalize so well.

Which? How much? When? Under what circumstances? To be replaced by what?

I don't know.

Only you do. In order to figure it out, you're going to have to think—all the time, and in critical, self-examining, humble, and open-minded ways. Make a list and keep adding to it. Ask those who know you to help you keep true to it.

I'm sorry for the ambiguity and the extensive homework. If you wanted the simple path, you should have picked up some other leadership book... I'm sure it has all the answers. This one knows the answers can only come from you and through you.

#4 Learn To Live Dangerously

How are you going to learn to do things differently? How will you ever become able to embrace the Power of Awkward?

You can't. You've proven that over and over. However, you can

<u>become</u> a person who can. Hence, we come to the transplant.

Most managers are taught always to be invincible, to have an answer for every question and to be poised, in control and "comfortable" under every circumstance.

That's you. You think you're a high flying risk taker because you wear a suit, drink lattes, and carry a Palm Pilot—but you're not! Haven't you noticed everyone else does, too? Like them, you live a life that is so safe; it's as if you never lived it at all.

If you only knew the terrific opportunities for learning and growth you pass up by masking your awkwardness, avoiding instability and traveling the same paths over and over, you might change.

I want you to change. I want you to begin to live dangerously. I want you to expose yourself to risk.

But let me be clear. By encouraging you to live dangerously, I am not recommending that you take up bungee jumping, rock climbing, or executive retreat rhinoceros hunting.

Leave the poor rhinos alone.

I'm talking about deliberately seeking planned, personal instability. It's the stuff that makes you grow and see the world differently. I'm asking you to plant yourself in environments in which you need to open your eyes and learn to become someone new. Become someone who is willing and eager to drop into specific situations that throw you off balance and destabilize your sense of control and comfort, make you think and act differently, and put you into contact with ideas, and ways, and points of view that you've never encountered. It may be ironic, but it's still true—only by becoming someone who does not always know what to do (and can be open about that), will you have a snowball's chance in hell of becoming the leader you're not.

Pack your bags. Get all your shots. Make sure your passport is still valid.

Learn to love traveling without a map. Believe it or not you can enjoy, conduct, and/or participate in a business meeting <u>without</u> an agenda. And you must.

(More) Excuses
(And {more} guarantees)

You'll have plenty of the former...

I have none of the latter.

I've told you that before, but it bears repeating... because you want it to be easy. Even now, you probably think I'm still kidding.

Let me state it even more bluntly.

If you're not sure that you:

a. Really want to change.
b. Are able to change.
c. Can follow through with the change you start; or
d. Can change over and over again.

Then... I have a piece of advice for overcoming that kind of challenge, one which I'd sincerely recommend you consider:

Stop Reading

This Book

Now

There's no shame in not going forward. There's not even any shame in not becoming a leader. There is shame in being a Moron Manager. Hopefully, since you've read seven chapters of this book so far, some of the things you've thought about will sink in and help you to be less destructive to others, even if you go no further. Because if you:

- Say you're going to change and don't; or
- Ask others for help and fail to act on their advice; or
- Pretend to change without really doing so; or
- Start changing and stop; or
- Change once and forget how to change again...

You will disappoint, hurt, and/or betray a lot of people around you. Please understand that this time, the pain you cause them will be even deeper than usual...

Because they started to hope in you again...
And hope betrayed is hope destroyed.

Even if you do change, there are no guarantees except one... a lot more work.

Choosing the tougher road does not mean you'll be rewarded for making that choice. I wish the world did recognize those who undertake heroic efforts and expose themselves to personal risk. With unparalleled career success, big financial payoffs and a ticker tape parade down the Canyon of Heroes.

But it doesn't. I can make a few promises though.

You will have the potential for a life that is more:

- Fulfilling
- Rewarding
- Invigorating
- Connected, and Meaningful

You'll be living, not role playing, and will have the potential to:

- Feel what it's like to have a significant impact on people
- Know that others truly respect, admire and care for and about you
- Share in <u>others'</u> growth and enthusiasm for life even as they share and contribute to <u>yours</u>

To drive home the point, let's do a value comparison…

Take the $100 million in stock options that a Moron Manager CEO might swindle and sneak out the back door with at the end of a long career. Sounds pretty good, but there is one potential disadvantage to it: that money is all in one company. It has no diversity. It's only numbers, but that may be what you want.

Compare it, however, to the variety of offerings included in the life portfolio of someone who chooses the **Interpersonal Change & Growth Fund**. The financial numbers may or may not be there… but you're sure to find genuine love, meaningful impact, abiding respect, deep admiration, and the coveted trust of others.

Putting aside any moral question of right or wrong, which would you honestly prefer?

At your retirement party, will the people come out because they have to or will they gather to say thanks and share stories of the memorable ways you touched their lives and impacted their own path?

Whether you make the senior executive team or are the school guidance counselor or the coach of the local girls' soccer team… how do you want to be remembered and what kind of impact do you want to have?

It will be easy to look back at the end and assess your success regardless of the course you decide to take.

Financial or career accomplishment can be measured in numbers and title… Did you make it?

There's only one clear way to tell if someone has been a leader in life…

Ask their followers

The Royal Road To Getting REAL
★ The Doctor Will See You Now ★

- ## Forewarned is forearmed.

    In your pursuit of getting REAL, focus first on changing your behavior... that which people notice first. Declare yourself. Proclaim to others that you are actively working on improving yourself! Forewarn them. Enjoin them in your cause.

- ## What gets measured gets done.

    Develop your own Personal Excellence Survey based on what matters most to you. Then, guaranteeing anonymity, ask "your people" to complete it honestly. Finally, sit down and share the results with them, warts and all. Enlist their help in helping you.

- ## Add REAL value.

    Ask your people to provide you with a list of what they really need from you. What are their core expectations? What are their true yearnings? Integrate those into your words and deeds.

Step 4

Getting REAL About Becoming a Leader Worth Following

Chapter Eight

The Power of Awkward
or
Repairing, Rebuilding and Rebranding To Become The Leader You're Not

So… you've done the Reverse Arm Cross exercise.

You've remembered what it was like to ride a bike the first time.

You understand that awkwardness is the essential feeling at the heart of all fresh, developmental experience—times that change who you are and how you act. It's just so damn difficult to love that feeling.

Ready to make it all REAL?

Andy Grove of Intel fame talks about Inflection Points—those periods in which a "company" is forced to make a choice between sticking with its old strategy and milking a mature market, or reinventing itself to become something completely new.

Well, that's fine for Andy, but let's talk about you.

On the path of life, Moments of Awkward are personal Inflection Points. They are the forks in the road, the choice between going the way that I've always gone that feels so comfortable and natural or taking the other path, the one that looks so dark and scary and feels so unlike me.

Which way is right? Hopefully, you'll have the courage, the mental acuity (the opposite of laziness), and the help of others (your people) to choose wisely. Here's a hint: If you are inclined to avoid a new direction because it makes you feel uncomfortable, anxious and not "who you are," you'd better give that path a good, long look. It might represent your last opportunity to become the leader you're not.

If, on the other hand, you let the "Barrier of Awkward" drive your choice and not try the new way, you've resisted a chance for growth and enthusiastically seized the opportunity to regress, capitulating to "who you are."

You've chosen to continue being who you are by following what feels safe… instead of taking a grand step forward towards insight and improvement.

Want an example?

What's the most awkward moment you've ever felt in your career thus far?

No, I'm not talking about the time you got caught in the copy room with an attractive colleague at the tail end of that really drunken Holiday Party.

I bet it was the day your boss walked over to your work station and gave you a tap on the shoulder. It was as if God were pointing his finger right at you, when you became anointed as supervisor of your own former colleagues.

Do you remember how strange that felt? Suddenly, probably overnight, you went from being a peer to one of the enemy. You had to talk with people differently, direct them, measure their performance, and control their activities—things you can't even manage with your own children, let alone a group of former friends.

It was traumatic and disruptive, and it was your own secret failing. You're not alone. Most people fail in that first transition. Companies are famous for filling a short-term gap that way. They take the person who is technically the best at something and make them a manager, without any guidance or developmental training that would help them succeed in an entirely new and highly visible role. They mistakenly and callously assume that skill transference from one level to the next actually works!

Here are your friends. You used to know how to talk to them about their problems, or their frustrations, or their goals... and now you can't because you're their manager. So, confronted with this tremendous change, you feel around in a panic for some clue as to how to behave now and the straw that you grasp for is the one that feels most natural.

You do what your bosses did to you.

You become cold, distant, authoritative, hard, infallible and also, as a result, defensive, manipulative, political, deceitful, self-aggrandizing and deluded. How enlightened! How motivating!

You could have made a different choice, but no one encouraged you, let alone showed you how, and so you end up doing what feels "right" in your eyes and the eyes of those supposed superiors.

Your people probably expected no more of you.

That doesn't mean they aren't disappointed.

The reason you chose "safe" is because you felt uncomfortable. Being comfortable only means you're stagnating, but that doesn't mean stagnating doesn't feel good or right.

Discomfort in a new situation, on the other hand, comes from two sources:

- An internal lack of familiarity with whatever it is you are doing; and
- The fact that people view the way you are currently acting as qualitatively different from how you've historically been with them.

So, here's your management career in a nutshell. A relatively unconscious series of choices designed to avoid feeling awkward. This time, however, when you're confronted with another Moment of Awkward, you're not going to get to use that same excuse again.

Feeling The Awkward
(Shifting to get comfortable)

It's time for another paradox.

In order to enjoy and benefit from those Moments of Awkward, you need to learn how to...

Become Comfortable

Huh?

Just when you were expecting this stuff to start making intuitive sense, there I go again, throwing another knuckle ball.

This is what I mean:

First, you need to become comfortable with the idea that you need a new version of you.

I hope you're not too surprised. After all, that is what this whole book has been about to this point. You may or may not be ready to understand yourself in such a meaningful, challenging way. Until you are, you're not going to be comfortable enough to move on and take REAL action.

Don't become a gutless procrastinator. Get over it. Do it anyway.

Second, you need to become comfortable with the idea that the new you is going to feel strange.

You expected otherwise? Wake up and get REAL!

Doing new things, being someone essentially different, will require that you overcome The Barrier of Awkward. Otherwise, you'll falter every time you decide to do or become something different, something inherently better.

You need to become comfortable with The Power of Awkward. To view feeling stupid and embarrassed as a huge blessing and a wonderful gift. You have to feel so open about it that you stop complete strangers on the street, grab them by the shoulders, stare into their eyes, and say,

"I'm doing something new! I'm becoming someone I'm not!"

And I love it.

I'm kidding, okay? I don't really recommend that you do that. As a matter of fact, do us all a favor and keep your enthusiasm to yourself until you decide to back up the new you with a sustained commitment to repair and rebuild the old you—otherwise it's just a narcissistic laser light show; pretty to look at, but signifying nothing. Besides, we all know that laser light shows haven't been hip since the 80's.

Next, you need to become comfortable with the people around you.

In many ways, of all the tasks and challenges you'll ever face in becoming the leader you're not, this seemingly benign and unremarkable one is the most important and difficult of all.

I'll tell you how soon enough. First, you should know why it's so difficult.

Because you've done a hell of a lot of damage to those people, and they no longer trust you. In fact, they probably don't even like you. It may even be the case that they are working actively against you right now, eager to see you crash and burn.

Ready to make them your respected colleagues, committed allies, and eager followers?

The Leadership Measuring Stick (No, not the one you use to hit your people)

Since we're in the game of accountability, let's come up with some measures of success in advance of our efforts.

No, I'm not talking about the way you measure success now. You know what I mean, those annual occasions when you meet with one of your people, discuss goals and come up with Key Performance Measures to assess their "progress." I know you're very comfortable doing that—after all, it's your ultimate secret weapon. Not only are you setting up the terms of your subordinate's potential failure and putting the onus on him to meet those expectations (without your developmental help)... but you're actually managing to make them contribute enthusiastically in their own trial and (if they fail) execution. What could be more fun than that?

If your people do fail... they hang themselves on their own goals... and you haven't done a thing to help them.

If your people do succeed... it probably means that you've met your group goals as well. As a result, you get to take all the credit for being a terrific manager. Still you haven't done a thing to help them.

The truth is your managerial goals and objectives are unobtainable by yourself. You are hugely dependent on the people around you to make them REAL. If you have a goal to increase sales by 40% over the previous year, no human could do that alone. Your success or failure depends on your ability to get the help of those around you.

That doesn't stop you from using their performance goals to blame them should you fail; or from taking all the credit if they happen to succeed. We went down that road before.

To measure your success as a leader, let's Get REAL about how your efforts and achievements should honestly be assessed. I propose that instead of hanging your people by their performance measures, they should hang you by yours.

Doesn't that seem fair to you? Well, too bad. That's the way it works whether you like it or not.

Here's why.

As with sales or productivity numbers, the personal growth goals and "leadership" expectations we're talking about cannot be met all on your own. You cannot become a leader in a vacuum. You need to have followers. In other words,

No Follower...

...No Leader

The question then becomes, not how many followers do you have, but what kind... because,

A Follower is not a passive sheep in a herd of other sheep.

A True Follower is someone you have enlisted voluntarily in a meaningful cause.

Don't believe me? Forget about the feelings you provoke in people; let's just look at the hard data of behaviors. In terms of what you elicit from your followers, there is a continuum of ways that they can respond to your "leadership." That will be our measuring stick.

Compliance

Most managers get nothing more and most corporations expect nothing less. However, there are two kinds, so let's take a look at each.

There's Passive Compliance or the "anything you say, boss" response which masks a feeling that goes something like this: "I think you're a complete idiot, but I know that you'll retaliate if I don't do exactly what you say, so I'll pretend to go along to your face." The moment people refer to you as their boss, you can be sure you failed them.

Then there's Blind Compliance, the kind in which people actually live under the fear of some kind of denigration or humiliation. They accept direction and march along despite knowing that they are contributing to a tragic mistake.

Most mediocre companies thrive on compliance. It's the air they breathe. It's what feels right and natural. Of course, management never takes responsibility for the atmosphere they've created when they decide there's a need to "shake things up." They merely set revised goals and objectives and kick-off a new spirit initiative. Such as: "The year of Success," "Pathways to Excellence," "Charging Ahead" and other trivial, hollow, meaningless slogans, printed at great expense on huge banners destined to become next year's toilet tissue! Then they wait at the other end of the tunnel with big clubs to see who fumbles.

Resistance

This is the bottom end of the continuum.

Resistance is usually passive. Most often you don't even know it's there until you discover the wound and learn that the bleeding is unstoppable. It's what happens when people say, "Yes, boss," to your face, but have zero intention of doing what they say they will.

Remember, that's <u>your</u> fault not theirs. No doubt, you're still having trouble with that concept.

There's also Active Resistance. That's when a company is at war with its own workers. Symptoms are manifold—but they can range from large scale voluntary resignations to theft, public slander, whistle-blowing, and sabotage.

It's rare, not because managers violate values so infrequently, but because people in general are so eager to accept authority that it takes an awful lot to push them over that edge.

Commitment

Finally, we look to the top end of the spectrum and examine commitment and what that means.

Tyrants and despots produce Resistance. Managers produce Compliance. Leaders produce Commitment.

The biggest difference between compliance and resistance is that resistance requires force and compliance requires surveillance.

Commitment, on the other hand, occurs when people have a sense that what they are doing is voluntary. They feel ownership over their own actions, and the success of their efforts matters deeply to them. As a result, they are more determined, creative, independent, and passionate about what they do.

Why?

Some people are just that way. Others need help. That's where leadership enters the equation.

The majority of people do things willingly and voluntarily not because they are committed to a particular cause—but because they are committed to a particular leader. In fact, they believe that if they do those things and act in those ways, they will actually BE LIKE THEIR LEADER.

That's what's known as Referent Power.

The leader serves as the referent for the follower. The follower acts as though they *are* the leader. It requires neither surveillance nor force, or even any direct interaction. In fact, a leader with Referent Power can influence millions without even meeting them, projecting his leadership persona into their souls. People look up to them. They watch them closely for indications of how to think, act, and feel. They want to be like them because doing so enables them, too.

Enlisting Followers
(By asking for their help)

Maybe that's why we confuse Leadership with strength, perfection, infallibility, and poise… that all knowing, all seeing personification of greatness who has all the answers and never needs any help.

There's no such mythical beast. In fact, it's a dangerous misconception of what it means to be a leader. It's probably one of the reasons why so many people try to claim leadership without actually being or acting leaderly.

After all, check out your own situation. You've thought of yourself, in some twisted way, as a Leader, but look at your followers…

Your department or group is mired in interpersonal pollution. Inadvertently, you've created a core of people who have your failure as one of their main goals. If they could openly add that to one of their Key Performance Measures of the year, they would.

Your management style has impacted people's lives in an unconsciously negative way, alienating and frustrating them in their own urge for development and improvement, disenfranchising them from the work they want to care about and be successful at.

How do you turn that around and make them your followers? Remember:

You can't do this alone,
you need their help to make you better.

The difficulty is, the people you need to make you a better leader, are your core supporters who already feel disenfranchised by your behavior. Becoming nice, all of a sudden, and asking those same people for help is going to make them more than suspicious—it's going to make them downright paranoid.

First of all, they've probably seen you undergo short-term behavior changes in the past. You know what I mean. You come back from vacation or from the birth of your child or from some communications workshop with an outside consultant... and for a little bit of time, you're like a whole new *you*. For all of 8.75 hours... or is it minutes?

Then you slip back to the old you, because ...guess what? "It feels natural." And why wouldn't it? That's the way you've been for 15 years. But here's the truth, Ruth,

You need to become Unnatural...
because Natural ain't so great.

I'm sorry that feels counter-comfortable and counter-intuitive, but so did your golf swing when the Club Pro got you to change your grip. Of course, you slipped back in to your old habits as soon as his back was turned. It's amazing, isn't it, how your score is still stuck in the mid 90s, despite all those lessons?

Here's another reason why it didn't stick when you changed your behavior the last time. None of your personality changes were born out of concern or empathy for other people… they all arose out of your own narcissistic sense of temporary self-fulfillment and personal satisfaction and short-term gain! It wasn't a better you; it was a further extension of how manipulative, arbitrary, and self-serving you are.

But your people are not as dumb as you'd like them to be. They knew you didn't mean it—even before you did.

If you really want to change and want that change to stick, this is what you need to do:

Repairing
(It's not just a quick check under the hood. It's a complete diagnostic and major overhaul of who you are.)

The first thing you need to do is repair the damage that you've caused.

Since you are probably in denial about who you are and how you've acted, you need to figure out what you've done wrong first.

Ask your people for the details. They'll know all about it.

This will be tricky and touchy stuff, to put it mildly, because the way most Moron Managers repair relationships is by firing people. Naturally, your people are going to suspect you when you ask them to describe the things that you do wrong. If they're smart and have survival instincts, instead of a Kamikaze-style death wish, they'll lie. After all, the first thing they're going to think to themselves is, "Why should I tell you anything like that. So you can identify where I'm most vulnerable?"

They might even tell you you're the best manager they've ever had, acknowledging reluctantly, that if you have any faults at all, it's only "little things" like showing up late for the odd meeting or forgetting the occasional performance review. They understand, however, and don't expect you to be able to do everything perfectly because you're carrying such a heavy load, you Hercules, you!

Here's a rule for you when it comes to the Repair Game: If other people around you are telling you how wonderful you are all the time.

Get new others!

Why? Because you really aren't hot, hot stuff. You still haven't managed to expose yourself to the truth… yet.

You need, instead, to promote an honest, clear, and detailed discussion of your failings. To do that, you need to let people know that it's okay for them to be open with you.

Repairing doesn't mean begging for forgiveness. That may be what you feel you should do, but while demeaning yourself before others may be good for your soul, it's probably not going to do anything for your reputation around the office.

Instead, there are three specific things that you need to repair. Acknowledge to yourself and your people that…

- I've got to repair *Me*
- I've got to begin to repair *Them*
- I've got to repair *Us*

If you're not willing to engage in that kind of triangulated healing, then don't begin. Most Moron Managers are only able to acknowledge Repair Job #2, "I've got to repair Them." They wonder, "How am I going to turn this person around?" Not, "What is it that I do that makes them respond this way?"

Remember, it has to start with you and be for you. Think of it not as "I need to *make* things better," but "I need to *get* better," as if you have some kind of illness from which you need help to recover.

It's not far from the truth.

Again, it's not going to be easy. You need to create a context that makes it both incredibly safe *and* worthwhile for your people to expose themselves to you, the person who has mauled and abused them in the past. You can elicit the rudiments of trust by guaranteeing that, as uncomfortable as this experience is going to feel, your intentions and, more importantly, your actions, will be healthy, helpful, and positive.

You can start this discussion on the right note by acknowledging that:

- You are not satisfied with the way you have been managing
- You have violated the bond with your people, that implicit contract between leader and follower

- You are aware that there are significant things you need to work on in order to get and be better
- You need their support in helping you get there

And most importantly, you need to promise that:

- You are going to take their advice and feedback in the beneficial and instructive way it's offered, not as a management ruse. That means, you'll really use it.
- You are prepared to make personal change and improvement an ongoing goal and will be open to both counsel and feedback about other issues as they arise in a life-long attempt to become the Leader You're Not. This is not a one-time quick fix, slap' em on the back, and send' em home happy personal initiative.

That covers how you can make it safe for your people to help you… but we still have to discuss why it's going to be worth anyone's while.

And, why would it be?

Because they care for you or feel for you or see the smallest part of you that they like enough to think you're worth saving?

Maybe. But not likely. Chances are, you're not even close to having that level of relationship with them.

If they do see it as being worthwhile, one of the reasons might be because they feel trapped in the relationship themselves. You're their boss. They're your employees. They have to live with you for the next number of years, so what the hell.

They might as well minimize the torture.

Rebuilding
(Rome wasn't built in a day, and neither were you.)

First, I have some bad news for you.

Engaging in overcoming the Barrier of Awkward and changing your behavior is not enough. Not by a long shot. Instead, you need to explain the reasons why you're making those changes in becoming the Leader You're Not.

That's the essence of rebuilding.

Huh?

Take a moment. Let it sink in for effect. I'll say it again.

The essence of rebuilding is explaining why you're doing it.

Just words, you sputter? What good are words? What about heroic actions, super human efforts, the ability to lift spirits as if you were lifting mountains?

I know. You thought we were going to invest six million dollars into the wreck of your life and receive bionic parts.

Did you imagine you were a star in a bad TV show?

If we've learned anything so far, it's that you are not who you think you are.

After all, your intentions are good.

It's your behavior that's atrocious.

The paradox is, changing your behavior requires internal changes first. Otherwise, the changes you make are not meaningful and won't stick.

You need to make the connections between intentions and actions absolutely solid and visible to you and everyone else if you're going to have a snowball's chance in hell.

Let's start by talking about you.

You're doing it for you because you need to rebuild your relationship with yourself. Without stating your intentions, you have no way of measuring where you are and how far you need to go.

Okay? Let's talk about everyone else.

You're doing this for everyone else because if you don't explain why you're changing your behavior, two things are going to happen: 1) People are going to think you've lost your marbles, and 2) You'll never know if you're succeeding or failing if you don't explain what your aims are in advance. They can't read your mind. If they try, they're going to assume all kinds of horrible things because of how bad you have been acting leaderly, at least up until now.

By making your intentions explicitly clear, you set them down for the record as observable yardsticks of success or failure. It's the only way you can get the help *and* understanding of the others who will be watching how well you meet those standards along the way.

So, get ready to start talking.

You're rebuilding in order to become more effective at what you do…

You need to say that.

You're rebuilding in order to relate to people as if they are human beings whose respect, encouragement, and support you must have in order to succeed.

You need to say that.

You're rebuilding because you've provided a disservice to the organization and your people.

You need to say that.

You're rebuilding because you've not lived up to your own expectations of who you could and want to be.

You need to say that.

You're rebuilding because there's so much more that you and your people could do together if you only give each other a chance.

You need to say that.

There are other, more personal things you need to say as well.

What about all the stuff you learned through talking to your employees and other important people in your life? You need to accept those things, figure out what you need to do better and differently to turn them around, then explain to others what your intentions and goals are in those areas.

You need to say that.

You might even have goals and ambitions as a leader, a desire to change things, help others grow, fill their needs, and improve the world.

You need to say that.

It begins with your words. The delineation of where you stand, what matters to you and where you need to go.

It's the only way you're going to get there. It's the only way you're ever going to get REAL.

Rebranding: Introducing the New You (Same as the old you?)

Most Moron Managers attempt to rebrand themselves without repairing or rebuilding themselves.

Given a healthy shock about their managerial failings, they come back to work in a new suit with a pressed-on smile and their hair parted on a different side. Then, they rearrange their office so that the room feels less foreboding and more open and friendly, or they replace the rectangular meeting table with a round one to show how interpersonally sensitive they've become.

However, moving the filing cabinet or wearing suspenders, ain't going to change your world, the world around you!

Moron Managers will try to learn a new language. They'll incorporate new words, starting with "please" and "thank you" and growing in sophistication from there. They'll say, "I see your point," when they really mean, "You call that idiotic sound bite a contribution?" Or, "I don't have a problem with that," when they really mean, "I've got a very large problem with that." They'll use politically correct terms like "empowerment" or "accountability" when they really mean, "Do what I say," and, "You'd better do it right." They become adept at meaningless, hackneyed phrases like, "We need to become more team-focused," or "values-driven," without having a clue what "team" or "values" really mean.

One remarkable thing about rebranding is that we can pick up on such hollowness and fakery in others almost immediately. For some reason, we don't think others can see through our own ridiculous costume.

REAL rebranding requires:

- Taking the information you obtained (through Repairing) about your own failings and incompetence

- Taking the values and intentions that you've made explicitly clear (through Rebuilding)
- Living this information, as though it is really who you are

It's not going to feel natural. Not at first. Others are going to think you're acting strange, even faking it. For a while, you actually are. That's what you do when you're learning something new, let alone learning how to become someone different.

In order to get better, you're going to need to press on through that feeling of awkward. Even when it feels like you're playing a role, stay the course. Even when it feels like the totally wrong thing to do in that situation, stick with it.

Remember what we discovered earlier,

Practice Makes Permanent

And practicing lousy habits makes for permanent lousy habits. But practicing getting REAL... makes you more real.

You've got to do it over and over again or else you lose it, even when people question your sincerity or mock your efforts.

It doesn't matter. In fact, that's when you forge ahead with even greater focus and resolve.

That's who you are. Someone you're not. Someone who is always in the process of becoming.

If they don't get it... too bad for them. You'll support them anyway.

Sailing for a New World
(By becoming the leader you're not)

You need a consciously intentional game plan. Your goal is to become a more respected and honored person: A Leader. The path you've chosen is not going to be easy… but that other path, the one that feels "natural," is the one that leads right back to where you started.

So, set out your new journey. Chart the course. Draw the anticipated obstacles on the map, your weaknesses and incompetence, your old habits, the traps you find yourself falling into again and again.

By laying it out, you might just stand a chance.

Along the way you're going to want to check to see if you are making progress. The best feedback you can get will come, not surprisingly, from others. The true gauge of how well you're doing is not necessarily the accomplishments you make, but that those you work with perceive what you're doing and how you're acting as…

- Voluntary (you're making a conscious choice)
- Meaningful (it matters to you)
- Sustainable (continuing to change will persist)
- Healthy (it helps you and others be better)

Without that kind of touchstone, chances are you're deluding yourself. Remember that you are always in the process of becoming the leader you're not, and that personal insight is not yet, nor may it ever be, one of your key virtues.

It's never going to feel easy or natural… except when it does. When that happens, do you know what that means?

You need to go to the next level. You need to figure out what to do next. Because,

It's not about becoming who you are…
it's about becoming who you're not…
again and again.

The Royal Road To Getting REAL
* The Heart of the Matter *

- **Embrace discomfort.**

  Self-conscious, awkward, uncomfortable, even painful... these are your best indications of REAL progress. Comfort = Complacency. You must outgrow your unconscious collusion with the past.

- **Abandon comfort.**

  Make a list of the tasks and activities which you love doing and feel most accomplished at... the ones which form the basis of your self-esteem and sense of grandeur. Now, delegate them to the people who work for you and find yourself a REAL leadership role.

- **Take the plunge.**

  Give a copy of this book or, at least this chapter to your boss. Have a conversation about it with him, charting a new course for your relationship and relative contributions.

Chapter Nine

....

Learning to Love
or
Hard Core Courage, Irreverence, Passion & Leadership Potency

It's not easy becoming a leader. My God, I have told you that enough times by now! We only act like it is and get horribly lost in the process. I wonder why. There are hundreds, perhaps thousands, of stupid books out there that all list the same simple ingredients, though their instructions on how to make the three tiered, icing-coated cake might differ in the particulars. Universally, they all understand that in order to become a revered leader, you need to learn how to:

- Trust your people
- Show them respect
- Acknowledge when they do well
- Treat them fairly
- Help them achieve the high standards and goals you set

Etcetera, ad nauseam, pardon me while I puke.

Sure, they're right. It's all true. You do need to show concern, be fair and treat people like decent human beings in order for you and them to achieve your goals. That doesn't mean that you will or that you know how, no matter how many books you read, courses you take or tapes you hear. You can take notes, memorize the concepts, listen to the gurus, draw the words "Trust" and "Respect" and "Accountability" in huge letters and tape them to the wall of your office or tattoo them to your forearms. It's still not going to get you there or change who you are...

Do you, by now, have the slightest clue why?

**Because all of those things are
focused externally,
on others...**

**Not internally,
on your self.**

That's right. Even now, when you thought we were getting to the good stuff like managerial strategy and motivation… it still comes down to fixing little old you. *You* need the strategy, not them; it's your motivation that's lacking, not theirs.

Don't feel bad, though; you're not alone. Most Moron Managers fail at becoming leaders because they have not established their own internal platform first. They don't know what they believe in or feel, so they can't even begin to impact what others believe in or feel in turn.

Make no mistake; what you and they *believe* and *feel* is what it's about, mate: the work, the effort, the commitment, the passion, the reverence, the intent, the satisfaction, the stamina, the persistence, the dedication, the creativity and the sense of accomplishment. It all comes down to what you and they believe and feel.

Do you not see that, yet? I know. You've got one hundred years of "management systems" shackles to throw off, and you're still not sure what it means to be free. You've become so used to the weight; you never knew the chains were there. While the rawness on your wrists is still fresh and painful, repeat after me so that you'll never forget…

> *They're not human capital…*
> *they're human beings.*

Say it over and over until you start to see the light. After all, your most compelling, overarching, elusive goal as leader is to genuinely "connect" with them.

If You Need to Manage Anything at All
(*It's still not what you think it is.*)

What we fail to remember when we think about managing other human beings is that we are emotional creatures, first and foremost. We have internal emotional systems, regulated, psychologically, and physiologically, through reactions to how we feel about things inside and outside of ourselves. Thus, the pre-eminence and validity of Daniel Goleman's concept of "Emotional" Intelligence versus "Cognitive" Intelligence.

In fact, it's our emotions, not our intellect, that drive everything we do and affect everything we feel. We only revert to the safety of our intellect when our emotional insights, sensitivities, awareness, and skill go into remission… which is far too often. One look at the business books, twenty minutes into an MBA program, a split second flipping through the most boring daily publication in the world, will illustrate to you how rare an insight the importance of emotional management is. We're told to think of people as if they are essentially rational, when they're not. In fact, it's a huge error, because when we get right down to it, what matters most to us as human beings, isn't rational at all. It's emotional.

Leaders know that. In fact, it might just be the only thing they truly need to know… and they know that, too.

That is why, if you are going to learn and practice how to manage anything in your career from now on, it will be this…

You are going to manage mood.

That's right, you heard me…

Mood.

Never thought of that one before, did you? Well, maybe that explains why you've missed the boat so completely in the past. In fact, your people know it's why you didn't find the right harbor.

If you manage Mood, you manage everything.

If you mismanage Mood, you mismanage everything.

It's as simple as that.

I'm not just talking about good moods and bad moods, though

that's part of it. I'm talking, in general, about what people care about, how they feel about what they're doing, who they're doing it with, and how they feel about themselves.

That drives what people do, and how well they do it, their contribution, their sense of commitment and passion... nothing else. It's not salary, not punishment, not measurements, not perks... not in so far as those things don't impact mood. Starting to see why those levers almost never work?

Here's the other trick.

First, you have to learn how to manage *your* mood, and then you have to learn how to manage *theirs*.

Did you think it would be otherwise, even after all you've learned so far? Well, you'd better not forget, ever. In fact, let's turn it into another chant, right here and now. Are those vocal chords still lubricated? Okay, you captains of industry, repeat after me:

First me...
then them.

Over and over.

Until you get it or until you don't even have to get it, to get it. Until it's the primary thing you think about driving to work in the morning, and the primary thing you think about on your way home:

How do I feel about what I did today?
How did I make <u>my people</u> feel about what they did?
What can I do differently to make it better tomorrow?

And the answers?

You get to fill in the blanks.

Your Internal Leadership Foundation
(Yes, I'm talking about yours.)

Leaders are REAL.

They are: One more time…

Responsible
Empowered / Empowering
Accountable
Loved / Loving

That's what they *do*. It's how they *act*. It's how they *behave*. It's how their deep sense of leadership expresses itself. It's also what they expect from others.

That's not how they got there or why they do it. That's not what fuels their behavior or their leaderly acts. That's not what drives them to lead themselves and others to be and become better. That's not what compels them to improve the world around them.

That energy comes from someplace deeper. A place that you, in your quest to become the leader you're not, need to access and proceed from the source of your very own leadership Mood.

The expressions of leadership demonstrated by Getting and Being REAL are based on three basic emotional states. These are common to *all* leaders and no true leader lacks any one of them. They compose the "Mood" that you must manage and nurture in yourself, if you want to become someone who cares about Getting and Being REAL.

Are you ready?

The emotional core of leadership is based on:

Irreverence

Courage, and

Passion

That's it. That's all you need to nurture. The rest flows out of that, is driven by it, and, can't help but occur without it.

Most Moron Managers avoid irreverence, courage, and passion like the plague because it requires them to commit to something other than a self-serving interest.

Leaders can't help but be leaderly because they embrace irrepressible irreverence, constant courage, and pervasive passion. They actively cultivate those emotions in themselves first and encourage them in others because the internal state of being that results compels a leader to be Responsible, Empowering, Accountable, and Loving.

Why?

There is no other meaningful outlet.

And to what end?

All in the service of *betterment*—making things (people, feelings, outcomes, etc.) better for you, for them, for us, and for the world. Yes, the world. Your world. When all is said and done, isn't that why you're here in the first place?

That's what leaders do and why.

Let's look at those emotions one by one and then together; you'll see how and why it couldn't be any other way.

Irreverence

Irreverence is about questioning convention, wondering why, and aiming a critical eye towards everything. Always!

With irreverence, nothing is sacred. It's about keen awareness of what is, diversity of perspective about what else is possible, and creative vision about what could be.

Being irreverent does not mean treating life in an off-handed way or being negative about everything. It simply means being unable to accept things as they are and unwilling to accept authority for the sake of authority.

Smoke that one!

You can't help it. That's the way you are. That's what you need to become.

Most of us don't think of irreverence as a virtue. In fact, most managers, parents, teachers, authority figures, organizations, religious institutions, and societies would stick a knife into irreverence in a heart-beat-given a dark alley and the chance of easy escape. In fact, that's what our socialization process typically strives to do!

It threatens the status quo—and self-interest. Because it questions the word from on high. It effects change.

That is what leadership is all about, the internal sense of irreverence that a leader uses to fuel a personal sense of *Responsibility* to make all those involved better.

However, be forewarned. One of the killers of irreverence is fear. That is why irreverence, in turn, drives the need for courage.

Courage

Courage is about taking meaningful, goal-directed action to change what irreverence identified as needing to be altered.

Courage drives a leader's sense of Empowerment and Accountability. It gives irreverence direction. If irreverence is "why" things need to change, then courage is "how" that change will occur.

Irreverence without courage is immaturity. It is the adolescent in the back of the class room, the smart-aleck, and the know-it-all in the team meeting. Courage without irreverence is simply bull-headed action, a force of direction that lacks the sensitivity and awareness to ask the simple yet incalculably powerful question "Why?"

While we're asking that question, let's ask it here, too. Why do you need courage to be a leader?

Because without it, you wilt. Followers have no reason to look up to you, and your "cause" becomes unreachable.

Make no mistake, feeling the responsibility to make things better, empowering yourself to take action and making yourself accountable for the way your actions affect the world and others is risky, scary, threatening, and even dangerous to you on a very personal level.

Uh, why?

Because "they" don't want you to, even if they say they do. In fact, "they" will try to stop you, discourage you, derail you, question you, dismiss you, ignore you, frighten you, or even threaten you to thwart you.

Who are they?

"They" are the enemy. "They" are the ones that everyone in the corporation talks about, the unidentifiable everyone "else" who caused the problems, ruined the business, put up the obstacles, or prevented the change. Don't let their phantom "they" status fool you. Whether "they" reside in the highest ranks or in the grassroots, "they" are out there, "they" are powerful, and "they" are resistant to you and who you are. "They" will do everything they can to stop you because they have a vested interest, no matter how shallow, meaningless, complacent, or perverse, in keeping things the way they are. In fact, the more "they" react, the more meaningful your pursuit!

Oh, them.

While we're at it, don't let the word "they" make you feel comfortable about "you." Because when you stop being irreverent and lose your courage, you become "they," an enemy of leadership and a spiritual Moron Manager. And the biggest source of "they" in you, is your own selfishness and self-interest. That's why the enemy of courage is social intelligence. Knowing what is correct or proper or self-advantageous, leads you to behave in ways that are appropriate, politically astute and counter to your irreverence. You end up supporting the status quo, rather than disrupting it, you cop out instead of leading the way.

Courage allows you to ignore all that and proceed, despite the risk, to do what needs to be done.

You see it, even when others don't.

It needs to happen.

If it doesn't, nothing will ever get better.

Passion

Passion is the key to Betterment—that irrepressible drive in leaders to create something better. If irreverence is "why" things need to change, and courage is "how" that change will occur, then passion is the "reason" the effort and risk are worth it.

Passion gives Irreverence and Courage purpose and meaning. Without all three, the drive towards betterment simply won't work...

Passion and Courage without Irreverence produces
Compliance.
Passion and Irreverence without Courage is
Pointless.
Passion without Courage and Irreverence leads to
Selfishness, Immaturity, and Narcissism.

Leaders view leadership as a social enterprise, not as an individual trait. Passion drives this and leads to Loving. It requires being loving about *yourself*, about what you are *doing*, and perhaps, most importantly, about those with whom you are doing it.

Using others to further your own goals without really caring about their betterment, their needs, their growth and satisfaction, is all about you. No leader will remain as one for long leading like that.

By definition, with REAL passion, you end up putting others first. Passion is anchored in the external world, not because you don't care about yourself or want what you want, but because what you want is not about you. It's not about you getting more, or you being promoted, or you securing power, or you succeeding. It's about you wanting to make something and/or someone better. If leadership is about inspiring people to surpass themselves, passion is the fire-starter.

Don't think for a minute that any of this altruism makes leadership a self-sacrificing act or a curbing of fundamental instincts. Just the opposite. True internal passion ensures that the way you behave is genuine, that you're not just playing a role. A leader wakes up in the morning eager to accomplish what needs to be accomplished in order to make things better. A leader is excited to work with others on that goal, feeling privileged for, rather than afflicted by, the opportunity to do so; happy to be living his life because it allows him to be who he is and who he needs to be to become a better person.

Consequently, Leaders are irreverent about what is, what could be, and passionate about the people who make it so.

That Three Tiered Cake Again
(With a cherry on top)

As this book draws to a close, I'd better make a confession.

I took a look at a bunch of leadership books the other day, standing in the airport book store, waiting for my thrice-delayed flight to be delayed once more. I said to myself, "Boy, I'd better make my own leadership book meaningful enough to get on 'Oprah' or 'Charlie Rose' or whomever will help me spread the message… otherwise I'm going to be slogging around the world, talking to small groups, waiting for delayed flights in non-hub cities for the rest of my natural life."

It was a horrifying thought, so I began flipping through the pages of non-fiction books, searching for whatever my leadership book still needed. I felt somehow, it was still missing something, the icing on the cake, a cherry on the top.

Then I found it. "That's it!" I called out in my excitement. The answer was right on the page. I almost licked it, the icing looked so tasty.

I picked up another book to be sure.

"There it is again!" I whooped and tossed that book aside to pick up another one.

"This one, too!" I yelled and threw it up into the air in my joy.

"They all have them," I explained to the security guard. "They all have diagrams!"

Really neat ones, too. With arrows and flow thingies and bedrock foundations and star-bursting epiphanies... the kind of drawings that make you feel leaderly just looking at them, all laid out, simple as a recipe, the answer before you:

> *"If I flow this way, rise that way, move up and back*
> *bi-directionally like that, dissolve into nothingness and then*
> *re-form as one of those...*
> *I'll be a Leader!"*

So, I thought, why should my book be any different? If they all have diagrams with flowing thingies, I need one, too.

Of course, I could see that those other books had dozens of models, pages of models, with zip arrows and line barriers and side angles and so many pools of collected stuff that my book felt as dry as Death Valley by comparison... and I knew I couldn't come up with more than one model to save my life.

But here it is. My proud creation. For *your* betterment... and "theirs."

I figure, if you've gotten this far, you deserve a Leadership Model that I built all on my own. If you catch me in an airport book store someday waiting for another delayed flight, I'll even autograph it for you.

TA DA!

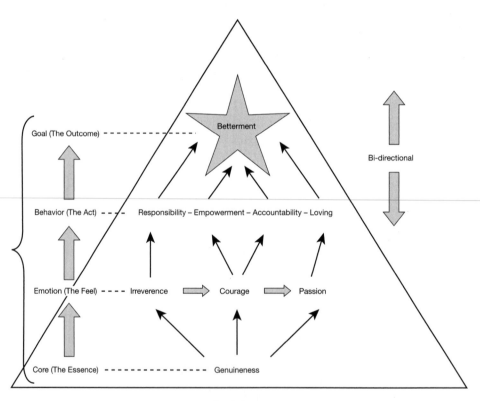

The How?

Notice how shrewd it is? How filled with arrows? How it leads to a star burst thingy, just like the very best?

At the bottom, is *Genuineness*. That's what you've been doing in becoming aware of who you are and how you affect others. It's the basis for understanding your own core values, what matters to you and why, what you're passionate about, what you won't sacrifice no matter how strong the temptation, and what you want to do and be in the world.

Those things have to be yours. You can't fake them. You can't borrow them or temporarily lease them or use them as a stepping stone to something else. It's just won't work.

Because, you see, not everything is worth doing or worth fighting for or worth a passionate commitment. We need to choose our battles as a way of choosing our way in life. We won't be able to feed ourselves emotionally otherwise. The only genuine way of knowing what to choose and what not to, is to understand and act on what's most important to us… a definable, concise set of core values which represent our ideals, and which no company can buy or steal.

What those values are is specific to each individual, but three aspects of them are common and expressed by all leaders:

- Other people matter more than anything else
- Making things better is a life-long pursuit
- It is as necessary to be loving to myself as it is to be loving to my followers

Next comes Irreverence, Courage, and Passion. We've talked about those and how they sequentially drive each other forward, and how they also must lead to Getting R*E*A*L. That's the link. Without that emotional fuel, that combustible mix in our own spiritual gas tanks, we wouldn't have the urge, let alone the need to behave as leaders with the people around us.

Excuse me for blowing my own horn, but that's a profound difference from the way we typically look at leadership or any human activity. Generally, we look only at behaviors for evidence of desired qualities and fail to recognize their source. A more holistic approach looks at how behaviors and emotions are connected, as well as how the behaviors of one person impact the emotions of another and so on, back and forth, bi-directionally. (See! I even worked in one of those reverse flow arrows, the same as those hollow guys do!)

That is why so many prescriptions based on explanations of what leaders actually do, fail to provide meaningful advice to those who want to emulate them. They don't demonstrate *why*. We end up, as a result, following rules and guidelines, playing a role, manipulating our own selves to act the way we feel we should in order to be more leaderly. Doing so means that we lack genuineness with ourselves and with others and come to rely on our ability to manipulate ourselves and others in turn in increasingly unhealthy ways.

Because of their irreverence, courage, and passion, leaders see themselves as proponents of a leadership model in which they:

- Feel **R**esponsible for others
- Actively do things to **E**mpower others and not disempower them
- Hold themselves **A**ccountable for the results of others
- Demonstrate **L**ove towards others and towards what they are doing

It's not a selfless act, neither on the part of the leader, nor on the part of the follower. Both sides are in it for something. In fact, that's the essence of why the relationship works so well.

Why are leaders REAL with others?

Because of what they get: accomplishment of a goal, the fulfillment of the dream and the realization of the condition that needs to be altered and made better.

Why do people follow leaders?

Because of what they get: satisfaction, recognition, true connection, improvement, an opportunity to see the value of their efforts come alive in the world through the process of what they are doing, and what is done for them.

Now comes the cherry on top. The reason for it all. The answer to the riddle "what for?"

Because, it makes things better for everyone.

Do you understand what I mean?

Irreverence causes you to see what needs to be changed. Courage allows you to take action to make that change occur. Passion is the reason the change is worth it.

Being Responsible, Empowering, Accountable, and Loving, is the way in which others are affected by you sufficiently to join your cause.

Your cause is in the service of Betterment-making the world, or your little corner of it better. You are working to enable a joyful, supportive, and successful place.

There's no doubt that to those who accomplish what they set out to do, rewards can come as a result. The payoff, recognition, and success often follow, but it's not done for those reasons, not by the true leader. No one follows a leader who only seeks their own betterment. It doesn't happen. Leaders are followed because their vision and efforts make the world and their followers better. And for those of you taking notes, irreverence is the source of vision, a necessary, yet oftentimes ignored source of inspiration for all of those corporate vision statements (albeit in a watered-down form).

Betterment means:

Doing well

by

doing good.

Does that sound alien to you? I'm not surprised. Because in most management situations, betterment means:

Doing well
by
doing badly.

In other words: Cutting corners, cheating customers, screwing colleagues, or otherwise acting in selfish, self-centered, self-benefiting ways, under the cover of darkness or in the guise of "enlightened management techniques."

It's why most of us, shackled by two hundred years of oppressive management tradition, fear that we will:

Do badly
by
doing well.

And, thus denigrate the Soft Stuff and pooh-pooh the whole notion of interpersonal sensitivity, self-awareness, and caring as core to our success.

If you want to be a leader, stick to the first definition and live by it. Your goal is Betterment. Doing good by doing well. That's your measurement, the definition of accomplishment.

Know that, in order for your leadership efforts to be successful, you need, when you look back upon them, to be able to say:

"I made things significantly better for myself and for others...
but not in that order!"

And the way you will know that this is true, is not because you think so... but because others do, and others tell you so!

Leading the Way
(To the status quo)

Without all three, Passion, Courage, and Irreverence, true leadership is not possible. You can probably see the evidence of this in the organizations that you have worked for or follow in the news. Not that organizations can have beating hearts, but they do take on the characteristics of their leaders and the people who follow them.

Some organizations actively embrace some of these emotional elements and disregard others. Think of the US Marines. No doubt, courage and passion are sincere values for that organization. Irreverence, on the other hand, probably lands you in the brig. Many cause-oriented organizations are the same way, from the Catholic Church, to the fundamentalist regimes of Afghanistan or Iran. Irreverence is just not tolerated.

Think of companies that value irreverence and passion, but seem to lack courage when it comes to putting themselves on the line; or others that seem, ironically, to have irreverence and courage but lack the passion to focus on any one particularly important thing.

I would argue that, in their early days, most successful companies enjoy the exact right mixture of irreverence, courage, and passion. It's what makes them so magical and brings visionaries and followers together with such commitment. It explains why they change the world, despite the odds, why they love who they are doing that with, and why they feel so good about the act of growing and becoming.

Some companies are able to keep that spirit. Southwest Airlines, those hideous busses with wings, had the courage and irreverence and passion to penetrate new markets with a new concept and treat people differently than their competitors; and they have been able to embody and sustain those values along with remarkable growth in a stagnant industry for 17 years.

Some companies, on the other hand, had it and lost it. The reason? The mixture changes, and the flame subsides.

When Irreverence flames out, an organization becomes insular and as part of the status quo, it cannot see change coming.

When Passion flames out, an organization becomes devoid of momentum (commonly called politics), and can't respond to the need for change.

When Courage flames out, an organization becomes afraid of losing what it has and can't do what it needs to do to change, the quintessential bureaucracy which stifles all things human.

Think of how Bill Gates and Microsoft conquered the world by seeing what others didn't. Yet, a deficiency in irreverence might explain why they were slow to the Internet, insisting until remarkably late in the game that it was not a very big deal. The courage and passion left behind might explain why Gates offended so many in their attempt to catch-up, including the US Government Anti-Trust Department.

Consider the wildly successful Wal-Mart, which is passionate about what it does and who it does it with, courageous about winning and being successful, but whose irreverence—the very source of its originality—seems to be dwindling as it grows, becoming more self-important, self-protective, and isolated.

A REAL Leader never buys into the status quo until they become the status quo. When that happens, they lose much of their leadership potential, succumbing to the pollutants of abject power. If they're true leaders, they take themselves out of the game (like smart entrepreneurs who leave their organizations at the $15—20M level).

Leaders talk about rejuvenating themselves to take on new battles, and yet so few pull it off successfully. They learn how to talk more passionately, or act more irreverently, or to be more courageous, but they never seem to be able to combine all three, perhaps because they don't see the link.

That's why you—someone who is becoming the leader you're not—must never forget that you are always, eternally becoming the leader you're not.

Over and over.

How Do You Start to Lead?
(If you don't already?)

Most people are not leaders because they are weak in one, if not all three of the emotional foundations of Irreverence, Courage, and Passion. If you're reading this book and taking notes in order to avoid or understand the potential derailment of your own career or life, I suspect this is your problem. So, for someone who feels that their sense of passion or courage or irreverence or any combination of the three is lacking or needs development, I have one piece of advice:

Start with the passion!

Work backwards from passion through courage and irreverence to drive what it means for you to get REAL.

That is, if you want to be a leader.

The first thing you have to ask yourself is,

"What am I really passionate about?"

Most managers can't answer that question. It doesn't even occur to them to ask in the first place. If you tried to pin them down to an answer under pressure, they'd make one up and fake it.

That's what it means to play a role.

If you, yourself, cannot answer that question, then I suggest that you don't pursue a leadership career.

There's no shame in that. Leadership is not for everyone. We're constantly fed the self-empowering mantra that anyone can be a leader—but it's not true. Sure, we can, but not effectively, or meaningfully, or enjoyably, or as part of a process of becoming someone we want to be. Anyone can fly in outer space, too, but should you be lacking the requisite skills, training and intuitive inclination, it helps, as a certain American recently proved, to have a spare twenty million dollars and a friend in the Russian space program. That's a lot of cash to fork over just to be passionate about something. Save that for the inheritors of family fortunes. Let them run their own companies into the ground.

What you've learned in this book will not go to waste. Being a better manager is infinitely superior to being a Moron Manager. If you practice the interpersonal skills you've picked up along the way, you will have a more positive impact on the people you work with and they will be grateful as a result... much more grateful, in fact, than if you announce your transformation into leader-hood and don't or can't see it through because your heart is not in it.

Don't feel bad about making that decision, should it become clear to you. You've come a long way to be able to assess yourself honestly enough to not fake something like that. You've saved yourself and others, and in the process, a lot of pain and heartbreak, confusion and frustration by being so candid. You've done well by not doing. So, give yourself a pat on the back. You are a better human being today. For that alone, you should be commended wholeheartedly by those around you.

If you know or come to know or want to know what you are passionate about, what alternative you want to create, use that emotion to fuel what it will take to become the leader you're not. That's what leaders do. They define what really matters first. Then they try to find out what matters most to others. They understand that passion has to flow back and forth and be mutually and individually meaningful in order to be REAL.

It's what drives a leader's curiosity and compassion for others. They make a conscious effort to know who they're working with and why those people are there, as opposed to just inheriting a workforce. They know that they alone do not have all the answers. They are genuinely concerned about others' well-being and interested in the idiosyncrasies that make them unique. Because they have that genuine empathy, they make sure they are aware of how those people see them and are affected by them. They treat them as allies not enemies, viewing them as a source of strength, rather than as a threat.

Passion is the key to it all, the fulcrum you use to move the heaviest of weights, the link between you and others and the things that need to be done.

If you feel at this stage in your life that these qualities have been beaten out of you, you are not alone. Management, as a science, has made that not only a systematic goal, but a holy cause because Irreverence, Courage, and Passion are the wellspring of insubordination and change… two of the Moron Managers' most coveted fears!

"They" would prefer that we get a Masters in Business *Administration* and develop management *systems* and define jobs as *functions* and treat human beings as dispensable containers of *capabilities*, and work for stakeholder value, and measure their balanced scorecard, and create a multitude of other dehumanizing, de-motivating, uninspirational destroyers of human and interpersonal potential.

How Irreverent is a policy manual or a business strategy?

How Courageous is a succession plan or an earnings statement?

How Passionate is a performance appraisal or an attempt to grow market share?

How much better do we make the world, our colleagues, and ourselves through what we do and the way we are doing it now?

A leader realizes that emotional moods do more to create the likelihood of success in achieving a goal than any guidelines in a policy manual or steps in a marketing strategy. A leader also recognizes that he cannot and never will be able to legislate emotions or passion or commitment or morale... or the myriad of other "soft stuff" which really matters. That's why a leader constantly manages his own mood state and how that impacts what others feel and believe. It's the only thing, in the end, that we can control and influence.

So, where do we go from here? Well, that's up to you. While I have to leave you now, hopefully, my message never will. It won't if you keep it in your heart and in your head, expressing it through your actions and your impact on others in all the things you choose to do from now until...

Forever.

By now, you know it's not easy and that it requires constant change and growth, ceaseless questioning, ever-vigilant thoughtfulness, and sensitivity.

Still, I have faith that you can do it, if only because you've shown the perseverance to make it this far. Your stamina, interest, and willingness to engage in such painful self-examination are a testament to your fortitude and the seriousness of your desire to get real. Real journeys are never easy ones. The mere fact that we've come this far together means that I care about you and your ongoing development into a real person. You've earned my faith, compassion and, dare I say... the "L" word (and I don't mean, "loathing," "llama," or "lust.")

As difficult as this journey is, hang in there and never lose hope. You now know that the secret to lasting change is not through rapid sweeps or grand pronouncements, but through real steps and concrete action. No matter how incremental those steps might seem or how insignificant their effects might appear, do not belittle the direction of your change for a moment. You are engaged in an endeavor that is heroic, meaningful, and compassionate, one that will be appreciated by the people whose lives you touch. Remember that fact in the spirit of the humility and critical self-awareness extolled by this book, even at those times when it feels as if you are swimming against the tide. The things you do to get real with yourself and others will be the things in your life that are most memorable. It's your legacy… your gift to the world.

While you're at it, enjoy the journey. The simple power and creative energy extended to those around us by embracing this way of being, is truly something wonderful to behold.

And have I mentioned that when it starts to become easy, you need to step back and figure out what you're doing wrong and how you can start the process all over in order to take it to the next level?

And have I mentioned that it's all in the service of others, never of or for you, even when it is?

No, it's not easy and it won't always be clear, but it might just be the most meaningful way you can spend the rest of your time on this planet. I believe that everyone can have an impact and create a better world around them, if only they aim to do so. And I know that you can, too.

But don't take my word for it. Others have said the same thing even better. Heed the words of Woodrow Wilson, instead. Let his profound comment be the last thing you read in this book, the last words that echo in your mind after you put it down and go back to your "normal" life:

Do not forget,
you are here to enrich the world.
And you impoverish yourself,
if you ever forget the errand.

The Royal Road To Getting REAL
* Leading A Life, Not Playing A Role *

- ### Who cares?
  Construct your own personal "What Matters Most Inventory." Identify three key items, all business-related and immutable to you and others. Then ask yourself how you have demonstrated their importance. Do others know it? You should care enough to fight for them regularly.

- ### Why me?
  Acknowledge and proclaim your self-interest. Let others know your own payoffs and theirs as a way to get beyond self-interest as a destructive force.

- ### To what end?
  Ask and answer... "What am I trying to make better?" "Why am I trying to make it better?" "Have I proclaimed this to my peers, staff, etc. in order to rally them to our cause?" Put a poster on your office/cubicle wall listing who and what you love and how you show it. Then make sure that you do... regularly and consistently.

He Bossed You Around for 200 Pages...
Meet the Author

Kenneth N. Siegel, Ph.D., A.B.P.P., is President of The Impact Group, Inc., a Los Angeles-based group of psychologists who consult with managers and executives. Dr. Siegel received a Bachelor of Arts in Psychology and Sociology from Rutgers University and a Master's Degree from the University of Southern California. Prior to completing a Post-Doctoral Internship in Psychoanalytic Psychotherapy at the Wright Institute, Los Angeles, he earned his Ph.D. at the University of Southern California, specializing in social psychology.

Dr. Siegel is married with three children and enjoys tennis, running and eating... but not necessarily in that order. ksiegel105@sbcglobal.net